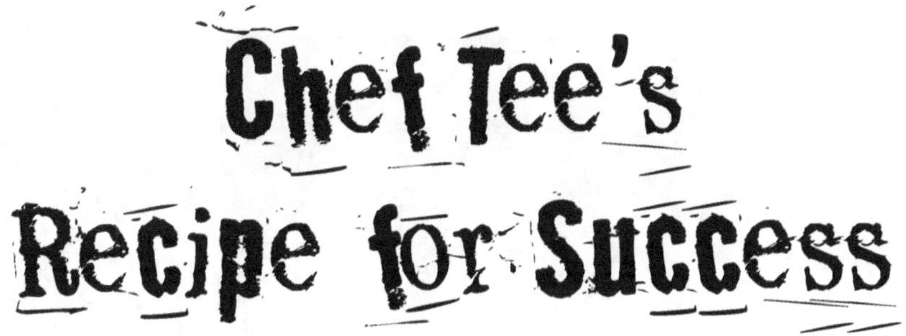

Chef Tee's Recipe for Success

A Recipe for a Successful Reentry

by Terrance "Chef Tee" Wallace
in collaboration with Jerry E. Bowser
and Julius E. Hoggard, B.A., M.B.A., QMHP

Visit the author's website at TurnAroundPlace.com

Published in the United States by Turn Around Place
Chesapeake, Virginia

CHEF T'S RECIPE FOR SUCCESS

Preface

With 637,400 prisoners released in 2012, research suggests that more than half (55.5%) of released prisoners will be (re)-incarcerated within 5 years (Durose, 2014). And a more recent research study suggests that there is a 44.9% recidivism rate within the first year of release and a whopping 83% recidivism rate for all parolees within their first 9 years of release (Mariel, 2018). As large numbers of individuals continue to return to the community from prison, policymakers and criminal justice practitioners continue to search for ways to help reintegrate offenders into the community and reduce the likelihood that they will return to criminal activity. With a forever changing political climate, a mind-set to "self-govern" is what the Returned Citizen, or the formerly incarcerated, must grow into. Most of our problems are rooted in how we define pain and pleasure. We, us criminally minded, define study as painful...as discomfort that is so unbearable that we would rather destroy our communities through the of selling drugs, forced prostitution, armed robberies, and the like. We'd rather scheme our way to wealth, as if that is possible, then to develop within the innate (natural) ability we were born with to succeed. We then embrace the beliefs that define pleasure as not working... not developing...not becoming. It is time to understand the truth: we are where we are because of who we are! And, if we want to change "where" we are…then, we must stop looking out the "window" and instead, look into the "mirror".

Chef Tee's Recipe for Success serves as a map and workbook for the Turnaround Place (TAP). TAP (https://www.turnaroundplace.com) is an organization that has been established to assist individuals who have experienced or are experiencing life challenges; however, these individuals have reached a point in their lives where they are ready to take a positive turn (a turnaround) towards improving their lives and achieving their personal best. TAP is committed to assisting/helping these individuals along their journey by providing resources that help them to TAP into their true potential. First, understand that the system was never created to "rehabilitate", "reform", "correct", or "transform" the imprisoned away from his or her "misdeeds" or "shortcomings". Only in understanding this truth and with self-determination, self- government, and self-directing will one truly succeed through the plethora of obstacles inherent within a system created to brandish a "felon" into a social caste system that literally locks him or her out of thousands of privileges and opportunities.

And, yet, at a time when our government is revamping an archaic system to offer reforming programming for those once tossed to the side without care, NOW is the time for those returning to become self-empowered with the mindset: if I AM to succeed... if I AM going to become the person that I was created to become, I must find the map to this destination. Well, welcome...for you have found it! So, read with a mind being a "cup half full" so that you may absorb the ideas as "tools" that may be added to your existing "toolbox". I'd say, "good luck", but we believe in making our own "luck". Both success and failure, are simply results. We believe that if you simply change the inputs then the results will change.

Introduction

Every day, we all get the same opportunities: a chance and a choice of what we do and with whom. The decision is on the individual, we can take the high road or the low road. Most of the time, we like to take short cuts or the low road because it's easier and it puts us right back at the starting line. Sometimes, we have driven so far off course we can't even get back in the race. If you have been granted this opportunity, it's up to you to try to fix your situation. Don't confuse it with support and responsibility. If you are lucky to have a support system in place, then thank God, because some of us don't have that support group and the ones that do, it's not fair for you to leave that burden to your support and say fix it. This is your responsibility as an adult.

Some of us go into a childish state of mind while in incarceration because we need, we want, and we want what we want right now. This is the reason most of us end up right back in prison. Because we failed to have a game plan. My journey from prison to society was not easy. God put it on my heart to share my story, the good, the bad, and the ugly. I've found a way through the wilderness of society to get back in the mainstream of life. I'm not saying this is the cure for your ailments or that this is the path to a better life. But I'm sharing my experiences and my Recipe to Success…

Your ability to self-govern will determine your level of success in life, business, education, and in leaving a legacy. Yes, your ability to dominate you! It's written that it's easier to conquer a kingdom than it is to conquer oneself. The first step to self-government is acknowledging the fact that ***YOU ARE WHERE YOU ARE BECAUSE OF WHO YOU ARE***, and if you are to go someplace different, then you must become someone different.

It's time for you to become the leader that your family, your community, your friends, and, most importantly, that you, need. No matter the condition of the person, the family, the neighborhood, or the culture…ultimately, someone led them there! Every person on earth is being guided, influenced, or unfortunately manipulated by someone whether directly or indirectly, consciously or unconsciously. Leadership is central in our world. So much so, that nothing happens without it; nothing succeeds without leadership; nothing is altered or transformed without leadership; nothing improves without leadership; nothing is corrected and nothing develops or advances without effective leadership.

What will it take for you to emerge as a successful leader in anything that you pursue? It will take discipline.

Discipline

To begin, it is essential that a leader determines their moral standards and writes them down in a declaration to others that "this is where I stand in times of feast and famine". This one act is easily accomplished, but it is the days to follow that will be the true test of time. Discipline is defined as "training that corrects, molds, or perfects the mental faculties or moral character" and "self-control" (Merriam-Webster, 2016). A person of character is disciplined in a sense that polices themself exercising control in accordance and parallel to your belief system. The problem occurs when your beliefs are corrupt, so then, your discipline will also be corrupted and lack the fortitude to persist through the challenges that invariably fall, for it is written, "It rains of the just and the unjust." This begs the question, when the storm and the rains come, will your foundation be of strong character, integrity, and moral fortitude to continue to stand? The answer will be found in your degree of discipline.

Strategic Thinking Skills

Perhaps the most important skill a leader needs is to be able to think strategically. Leadership is all about having a vision of where you want to be and working to manifest that vision. But what does 'strategic thinking' really mean, and how can you develop strategic thinking skills? Strategy, in its simplest sense, is deciding where you want to be and how you're going to get there, and then taking the action necessary to do so.

What do you need to do to develop a strategy?

- It sounds obvious but, as a first step, you need to know *where you are now.* Everything that you do starts from your current position. Even in the nursery rhyme, Grand Old Duke of York, whose skill in maneuvering has gone down in history, or at least nursery rhyme, couldn't move downhill until he had first moved up. So, gather as much information as you can about where you really are and don't accept anecdotes as truth. Demand evidence. The crucial element is to see where you are now and *not worse than you are.*

- Next, *identify the ideal future position at a particular point in time.* This could be in five years, ten years, or one year's time, depending on the situation. There are lots of tools out there for doing this in workshops, including visualization, drawing pictures, 'blue sky' thinking and so on, but you can also just spend time thinking about it. Visualize yourself and write these goals down and hang them where you can see it. That is EXACTLY what I did within the first 60 days home. I learned this from an acquaintance when I witnessed a large dry board on her wall with short-term and long-term goals. Step-by-step, like a mathematical equation that translates into a solution, or the intended goal. I literally mapped out my educational pursuits and looked up years later to see the solution manifested by sticking to the steps. It's important to aim high at this stage, but also to be *as detailed as possible.* The more detail you can include, the more you know what you want, whether at home or at work. And it's much more concrete on paper. And never forget, that what you were designed to become, will initially, scare you because it will be much greater than you can accomplish alone.

- Now, from your ideal future position, think about what is really important to you. *Where do you or where does it really need to be?* This is about prioritization. Pare your essential position down to the bones, so that you are really clear what is crucial. Highlight the top three issues or elements, then the top five. Identify any details, which really don't matter. This is why you needed lots of detail at the last step: you can now pick out which details are really important.

- Now it's time to *work out the intermediate milestones from 'now' to 'then'.* Now you know where you need to be in five years' time, where would you need to be in one, two, or three years in order to get there? Concentrate on 'milestones' rather than 'actions', that is, things you will have achieved, rather than what you're going to do in practical terms.

- Finally, it's time to *work out actions:* what you need to do to get from 'now' to your first intermediate milestone, then from there to the next and so on.

THE FINAL ELEMENT OF LEADERSHIP

- **Keeping your Strategy on Track.** Having a strategy is all very well. Achieving it is quite another issue. This is what really marks good strategic thinkers out from others: everything that they do contributes to their strategy, or at least, does not actively work against it. Before they make a decision, they consider how the possible outcomes fit into their overall strategy. If it doesn't fit, they don't do it! And if they really want to do it, and it doesn't fit with their strategy, they review their strategy to see if it's still appropriate.

It's worth taking a bit of time every so often, perhaps once every six months to a year, to review your strategy, and make sure it's still right for you or the company, and also that what you are doing is contributing to your strategy. As a business leader, a company away-day is a good opportunity to do this, although many companies use board meetings as a regular chance to review strategy.

At home it can be harder to find the time, but it's still worthwhile. Sit down with a cup of tea or coffee, and just look at where you wanted to be, and how you thought you'd get there. Is it all still valid, or do you need to tweak it a bit in view of changes to your life? And what difference does that make to what you're doing every day? Regular updating keeps it fresh in your mind and shows that you're still committed to the overall picture, which makes it easier to make any changes in your day-to-day life needed to achieve your goals.

Chapter 1 - Challenges

For the average returned citizen, pre-imprisonment entailed trauma on different levels, and different degrees, but, nonetheless, trauma that has yet to be healed. Many of these hurts and pains were absorbed during child and adolescent years and never dealt with because you were called to be an adult too early...and, unjustly so. Then adding the prison environment to an already traumatized young mind, what develops is yet unknown. However, recent studies of the effects of re-entry show that funneling "felons" to certain zip codes that accept such brandished social castes has developed subcultures that are embracing and reproducing in those around them (the youth). A "legal cynicism" that views the "system" at large (including the educational fabric that leads to higher earning power) as a "scam". It is separate from us and not inclusionary for us and begs the inherent question within this group, "why bother to play by rules that do not serve us?" (Kirk, 2016)

What does this mean? This means that those coming home from prison and strategically placed in the only neighborhoods zoned to accept felons, impoverished areas, are having a negative impact on the pro-social culture that exists in that area and are negatively affecting the community. What this means is that we who have experienced imprisonment have allowed the values, customs, and culture of prison to permeate our minds' beliefs, thoughts, and, invariably, our behavior. "Like begets like," that is, an apple tree gives forth an apple...So, too, the hardened, aggressive, and violent prison culture that is a "culture of honor" is pouring out people who, unconsciously, have forgotten who they are...and, by their very nature, who they are supposed to become.

So, what are we, the formerly incarcerated, to do? First, we must examine what we believe. Transformation can only come about from within...and, in that inner transformation you will find your purpose...your reason...your why for all that you've been through. There is no "coincidence" in the trials, tribulations, and challenges that have fallen on most of us that have walked the prison yards wondering, "why all this pain...why all this struggle?" The "silver lining" in it all...in your pain is in the The Law of Harvest, which states that you reap what you sow. In other words: the depths of your pain is equal to the potential heights of your strengths. You have endured and left alone will soon atrophy. This is the critical variable in the attainment of new skills – in developing ourselves and others. It is our ability to stay persistent even when we are unable to see any growth on the surface….just like the Chinese Bamboo Tree.

The Challenge We Learn from the Chinese Bamboo Tree:

Can we stay focused and continue to believe in what we are doing even when we don't see immediate results? Will you believe in your vision and goals even when everyone around you is criticizing your lack of visible results?

Law #7: We can't do Anything about Last Year's Harvest, but We can about this Year's!

Life is full of consequences both empowering and disempowering. The most important choices are often the ones that seem small by comparison, yet they all center on how you choose to use your time. Never forget, what you do in the dark is what you will be praised for in the light. But how do you handle it when last year's harvest is not so good, when you have fumbled the ball or failed? The tendency is to let our failure keep us from positive sowing today. What you must understand and act on is this final law of the harvest—you cannot do anything about last year's harvest, but you can surely do something about these years ahead of us. This law translates into at least four important concepts that you must understand and apply:

1. We cannot do anything about last year's harvest.

2. We must learn to live with the consequences of our failures so forgive (let go) all the failures that were done by you and "to you". Embrace the belief that nothing has happened to you but for you in this process called life. This belief will empower you.

3. We must commit ourselves to this year's harvest.

4. We must not judge our harvest by the standards of the world and its ideas of success but hold onto the vision that you have, because you will certainly succeed. However, your success is up to you, to put in the work of consistent intentional personal development that will help you to "fail forward" instead of just failing.

CONCLUSION:

The Social Exchange Theory, based on proven data that social behavior is the result of an exchange process. The purpose of this exchange is to maximize benefits and minimize costs. According to this theory, developed by sociologist George Homans, people weigh the potential benefits and risks of social relationships (Baumer, 2007).

The prison environment conditioned you to isolate and disconnect from the social world around you because that is the socially acceptable norms and customs of that sub-culture, which is not normal or sustainable because you were not created to harm people or yourself. Now you must understand that the world, community, and people will only give you what you give them in fair and equal exchange. So, your power is in the acceptance and action of this principle of social exchange. Give what you desire to receive. The social sciences promote a concept and theory called the Self-fulfilling Prophecy.

The Self-fulfilling Prophecy is a belief that comes true because we are acting if is already true (Merton, 1948). New Agers call this The Law of Attraction, but there is nothing mystical about it. Our expectation that we will see a particular outcome changes our behavior (see above diagram), which shapes the way others see us. In turn, the feedback we get from the others and the world around us, serves to reinforce the original belief that leads to the change in behavior.

FORGIVENESS CREATES ROOM FOR BETTER THINGS

The "Illinois Medical Journal" carried an article that states why this (learning to forget the past, etc.) is so important (Puchalsk, 2009). There are two days in every week about which we should not worry—two days, which should be kept from fear and apprehension. One of these days is **YESTERDAY** with its mistakes and cares, its aches and pains, its faults and blunders. Yesterday has passed forever beyond our control. All the money in the world cannot bring back yesterday.

We cannot undo a single act we performed; we cannot erase a single word we said. Yesterday is gone. The other day we should not worry about is **TOMORROW** with its adversities, its burdens, its large promise and poor performance. Tomorrow is beyond our immediate control. Tomorrow's sun will rise either in splendor or behind a mask of clouds—but it will rise. Until it does, we have no stake in tomorrow, for it is as yet unborn. That leaves only one day—**TODAY**. It is not the experience of today that drives men mad—it is remorse or bitterness for something, which happened yesterday, and the dread of what tomorrow may bring.

When you live in regret about the past or worry (anxiety is being anxious about what has yet, or never will, occur) about the future, you rob yourself of your only power: the present moment. And, when you take away that power, you endanger the future. By taking care of today we provide for tomorrow—or at least prepare for it. And success is 90% preparation and 10% opportunity. The question is not whether you will get another opportunity, but rather, the question is: how prepared will you be when the next opportunity comes?

In the book, The Art of War, it says that if you prepare for 100 battles out of 100 then you will be successful in all 100 battles. Your reintegration will be a battle that will be fought first internally and then externally. Yet, whether you "win" (reach your true potential) will be determined on how you respond to the internal battle, first, then, externally. The more you prepare yourself with the skills, tools, and habits that empower you, then the more successful you will be personally and professionally throughout your reintegration.

What value can you add to the world? What value can you add to the world around you... now?

Chapter 2 – Assets & Resources

TIME

The greatest resource we have, when viewed in terms of its scarcity, is time. Our world perceives time as so important and valuable that when we violate a law severe enough, we are placed on time out, or imprisoned. Time is so valuable (and limited) that from the moment that we are born, we are running out of time (dying).

We are losing seconds, minutes, hours, days, and years from a destined timeline long enough for us to become the solution to a problem. Your time in prison can be seen as wasteful or useful; it's all a matter of perspective. I witnessed a pattern amongst those who failed and those who succeeded through reentry: those who utilized their time by gaining skills and tools through personal development (reading, programs, proper fellowship) are the ones that successfully created a better quality of life upon successfully completing reentry. Those who waste their time tend to adopt a mindset that their "imprisonment was a waste, the system is unjust, and everyone is corrupt." Such self-destructive talk is common amongst those returning, consequently, the extremely high recidivism rate.

RESOURCES VS. RESOURCEFULNESS

If you are to succeed in reentering society and creating a quality of life that you deserve, then you must understand that it is not about resources, but rather, it's about your resilience and tenacity to be resourceful. In 1995, at the age of 16, I was charged with felony murder and armed robbery. Placed in solitary confinement for 387 days as I challenged two trials, I studied day and night, books of all kinds. As previously discussed, the word education stems from the root word educer, which is Latin meaning, "to lead (draw) out of something or someone" (Merriam-Webster, 2016). True education is a leading out of what is already within you; it's simply a reminder of what you already inherently know. True education is letting go of the dysfunction that your past environments conditioned you to and embracing your true self made of love and from love. You have access to infinite intelligence that possesses an unconscious power. Once you understand that you are creating your own reality, only then will you be empowered to intentionally and strategically shape that reality.

ATTITUDE

Your attitude determines your altitude. Period. Why? Because attitude is defined as "a state of mind," and when our state of mind believes that the world, those around you, life, the universe, or God has somehow "shortchanged you" then we begin to reinforce an attitude of ungratefulness that affects every single encounter that we have.

So, you will begin to sow bitter seeds that perpetuate the bitter fruit, unaware that it is you who are creating your unwanted reality. And, the truth is, our most important resources are the daily connections that fate brings our way. Only when my mindset shifted, was I able to take advantage of the opportunity before me. The opportunity for accredited schooling ended because of a lack of money (resources), and yet, who I became in the process allowed me to be resourceful. Don't squander your opportunities because of a bad attitude! My attitude at 17 was that of a quitter with no vision. I missed out on walking out of prison with a bachelor's degree because of it.

Think about what opportunities are in front of you that you are squandering.

FAMILY & FRIENDS

Who you wish to become and who you are really rests upon who and what you allow into your circle of influence. So be very cautious of who you surround yourself with. Seek positive, goal-oriented, purpose-driven people who are chasing something greater than themselves.

For most of us who have served years imprisoned, we will just begin to understand the trauma we have endured. Since we will just begin the conscious unravelling of the layers of trauma imparted upon our minds and hearts, do not expect your family and friends to truly understand all that you have gone through. It is a process for both you and them, so be patient and understanding with yourself and with them. They'll find it difficult to understand the deep trauma suppressed in your subconscious so that you could cope and deal with problems that were more pressing, and time-sensitive, such as protecting yourself when you talked on a prison yard phone, showering, or simply sleeping.

The challenge, upon reentry, exists in the fact that you have been conditioned to "win" every fight, whether verbal or physical. In prison, weakness is preyed upon. This environment conditions you to resolve all conflict with violence and aggression as a means to protect yourself for the long term. What I did not understand at the time was that conflict is inevitable and, although some problems may be described as a "nail", not all are. And, when the only solution you have is a "hammer", then all conflicts will look like a "nail".

Prison is a war zone with no "barracks" to rest and recover before having to go back out into the battlefield. No, prison in its entirety, is a battlefield whose war wages without end both mentally and emotionally, and surfaces on the physical plain periodically. Yet, it is the incessant threat of violence that leaves a lasting imprint of trauma on the psyche of the imprisoned. You survived prison by learning and being conditioned to wield the "hammer", yet reentry demands for you to utilize different techniques to respond to the conflicts of everyday life.

For example, living at your family's house, or significant other, and facing the challenges of sharing a living space whose rules of engagement are completely opposite from the prison environment. If you respond with the "hammer" to your child, mother, or wife then you will traumatize them, just as you were traumatized. And that trauma will plant a seed of distrust between you and the family member or friend. It will condition them to view you as violent, unstable, and not to be trusted, when in fact you are conditioned to respond to all stress aggressively and violently because that is the "tool" that helped you succeed (stay alive) all these past years. The challenge to overcome is that reentry will entail everything new, from ordering food from a menu to grocery shopping, which will trigger your autonomic nervous systems' fight or flight automatic response. Unfortunately, you've been programmed to respond with aggression, yet, understanding these challenges before walking into them will empower you and your support system during your reintegration.

Yes, recovery for the formerly incarcerated, in many ways, is a traumatized patient trying to recover from years of mental, emotional, and physical abuse. However, the returning citizen must be consistently aware that trauma, pain, and unhealed wounds have also resulted in the lives of those closest to us and, as a result of our terrible choices that harmed the community, ourselves, and, unfortunately, the ones we are coming home to.

In most cases, there exists severe trauma that has yet to be expressed because of the structured setting of prison, the lack of resources to communicate because of the high costs for phone calls, and the long distance in relation to most prison complexes that have been built in rural America while the prisoners come from the inner cities.

Your release will peel back scabs for family members that have harbored and held back emotions because the time, place, and connectedness did not provide the space to do so. Yet, now you are home. Now, there is no 15-minute time limit on a phone call, so how will you respond when your mother, grandmother, sister, or daughter is expressing unceasingly their pain and heartache because of what you did. The greatest challenge will be in listening, accepting, and responding in a way that validates how they feel so that those wounds may heal. Take this opportunity to listen, validate, and apologize for the pain you caused. It will help in your healing and success in reentry and in healing those that will be your biggest supporters. Feed those who feed you.

MENTORS

For those who are unaware, the criminal justice system continues to carry a culture of separatism. For example, in every prison diner in the Michigan Department of Corrections, there is an unwritten "Black Side" and "White Side" that most adhere to. This narrow mindedness creates a narrow networking system and, in a world where relationships govern success and failure, a small network usually translates into a small net worth. To maintain a mentality that, "because I am black then only a Black Mentor may help me" reduces my resources exponentially.

"The word Mentor is derived from the Greek Mythical story of The Odyssey where a man named Odysseus went on a journey (odyssey) of 20 years. Before going, he asked his trusted teacher and counselor, Mentor, to be responsible for the raising of his young son. Thus, originates the word, mentor."

(Bueno, 2018)

Imprisonment, unfortunately, strips of the understanding that you are part of a collective, of a greater whole. You are stripped of the understanding of the power of leveraging diversity. It pits one man against another, dividing and conquering both internally and externally, the returning citizen must reconnect with that inner understanding that what we do to another, we invariably do to ourselves. In order to survive, we became hyper paranoid and create walls that separate us from the whole, unconsciously destroying our ability to empathize, sympathize, and, preventing you from being fully humanized.

Leveraging diversity means being able to create and develop opportunities through different kinds of people while recognizing and celebrating that we all bring something different to the table. It requires that you destroy those layers of callousness created through trauma that helped you survive the emotional and mental turmoil that results from incarceration, but it will, invariably, only block you from the blessings of mentors that will pour into your life as you go further on your journey to becoming the person you are supposed to become. Each new dimension (level) will require a new mentor that may lead you from, and through, a place that they themselves have travelled. Be open as a "cup half full" so that you may walk into new spaces with a capacity to be "poured into" thereby leaving each experience "fuller". We must accept the reality that we don't always have the best answer, a requirement that prison thrusted upon your back in order to survive because, in most cases, we had to be our own most trusted counselors.

"Leveraging diversity does not mean that you treat everyone in exactly the same way, but that you tailor the way you interact with others to fit with their needs and feelings."

(Goleman, 1995)

Just as imprisonment involved a process of finding a productive routine while gaining the social skills, customs, and etiquette, a similar routine will be needed. You must go into this new journey with a cup half full mentality, your desire to be filled with skills, tools, and loving relationships that are now here to help you help yourself. Seek mentors that specialize in the field of industry or study for which you desire and have mapped out to pursue because they have experienced the obstacles that you may come to face, thus, a wise man learns from others' mistakes. Find a mentor that is accomplishing what you seek to accomplish and they will help provide the map that will take you where you need to go much quicker, with fewer mistakes (less time & money lost) and help to expand your network (relationships).

Remember, it is not what you get, but who you become that matters, Process over Product, because you attract what and who you are. So, the goal and focus are personal, self-development that will result in a "better you" attracting a better life. It is essential to understand this if you are to benefit from mentoring relationships because many will come by way of you giving first with the belief, through the understanding of the Universal Laws & Principles, that what you give will be given back to you, multiplied.

Chapter 3 – Relationships

THE ORIGINS OF YOUR RELATIONSHIP: ATTACHMENT, BONDING, AND RELATIONSHIPS

You were born preprogrammed to bond with one very significant person—your primary caregiver, your mother. Like all infants, you were a bundle of emotions—intensely experiencing fear, anger, sadness, and joy. The emotional attachment that grew between you and your caregiver was the first interactive relationship of your life, and it depended upon nonverbal communication. The bonding you experienced determined how you would relate to other people throughout your life, because it established the foundation for all verbal and nonverbal communication in your future relationships.

Individuals who experience confusing, frightening, or broken emotional communications during their infancy often grow into adults who have difficulty understanding their own emotions and the feelings of others. This limits their ability to build or maintain successful relationships. Attachment—the relationship between infants and their primary caregivers—is responsible for:

1. Shaping the success or failure of future intimate relationships.
2. The ability to maintain emotional balance.
3. The ability to enjoy being yourself and to find satisfaction in being with others.
4. The ability to rebound from disappointment, discouragement, and misfortune.

Scientific study of the brain—and the role attachment plays in shaping it—has given us a new basis for understanding why vast numbers of people have great difficulty in communicating with the most important individuals in their work and love lives. Once, we could only use guesswork to try and determine why important relationships never evolved, developed chronic problems, or fell apart. Now, thanks to new insights into brain development, we can understand what it takes to help build and nurture productive and meaningful relationships at home and at work.

What is the attachment bond?

The mother-child bond is the primary force in infant development, according to the **attachment bond theory** pioneered by English psychiatrist John Bowlby and American psychologist Mary Ainsworth.

The attachment bond theory states that the relationship between infants and primary caretakers is responsible for:

1. Shaping all of our future relationships.
2. Strengthening or damaging our abilities to focus, be conscious of our feelings, and calm ourselves.
3. The ability to bounce back from misfortune.

Research reveals the infant/adult interactions that result in a successful, secure attachment, are those where both mother and infant can sense the other's feelings and emotions. In other words, an infant feels safe and understood when the mother responds to their cries and accurately interprets their changing needs. Unsuccessful or insecure attachment occurs when there is a failure in this communication of feelings.

Researchers found that successful adult relationships depend on the ability to:

- Manage stress
- Stay "tuned in" with emotions
- Use communicative body language
- Be playful in a mutually engaging manner
- Be readily forgiving, relinquishing grudges

The same research also found that an insecure attachment may be caused by abuse, but it is just as likely to be caused by isolation or loneliness. These discoveries offer a new glimpse into successful love relationships, providing the keys to identifying and repairing a love relationship that is on the rocks.

The attachment bond shapes an infant's brain.

For better or worse, the infant brain is profoundly influenced by the attachment bond—a baby's first love relationship. When the primary caretaker can manage personal stress, calm the infant, communicate through emotion, share joy, and forgive easily, the young child's nervous system becomes "securely attached." The strong foundation of a secure attachment bond enables the child to be self-confident, trusting, hopeful, and comfortable in the face of conflict. As an adult, he or she will be flexible, creative, hopeful, and optimistic.

Our secure attachment bond shapes our abilities to:

- Feel safe

- Develop meaningful connections with others

- Explore our world

- Deal with stress

- Balance emotions

- Experience comfort and security

- Make sense of our lives

- Create positive memories and expectations of relationships

Attachment bonds are as unique as we are. Primary caretakers don't have to be perfect. They do not have to always be in tune with their infants' emotions, but it helps if they are emotionally available a majority of the time.

Insecure attachment affects adult relationships:

Insecurity can be a significant problem in our lives and it takes root when an infant's attachment bond fails to provide the child with sufficient structure, recognition, understanding, safety, and mutual accord. These insecurities may lead us to:

- Tune out and turn off – If our parent is unavailable and self-absorbed, we may— as children—get lost in our own inner world, avoiding any close, emotional connections. As adults, we may become physically and emotionally distant in relationships.

- Remain insecure – If we have a parent who is inconsistent or intrusive, it's likely we will become anxious and fearful, never knowing what to expect. As adults, we may be available one moment and rejecting the next.

- Become disorganized, aggressive and angry – When our early needs for emotional closeness go unfulfilled, or when a parent's behavior is a source of disorientation or terror, problems are sure to follow. As adults, we may not love easily and may be insensitive to the needs of our partner.

- Develop slowly – Such delays manifest themselves as deficits and result in subsequent physical and mental health problems, and social and learning disabilities.

Causes of Insecure Attachment

- Major causes of insecure attachments include:
- Physical neglect – poor nutrition, insufficient exercise, and neglect of medical issues
- Emotional neglect or emotional abuse – little attention paid to child, little or no effort to understand child's feelings, and verbal abuse
- Physical or sexual abuse – physical injury or violation
- Separation from primary caregiver – due to illness, death, divorce, adoption
- Inconsistency in primary caregiver – succession of nannies or staff at daycare centers
- Frequent moves or placements – constantly changing environment; for example: children who spend their early years in orphanages or who move from foster home to foster home
- Traumatic experiences – serious illnesses or accidents
- Maternal depression – withdrawal from maternal role due to isolation, lack of social support, hormonal problems
- Maternal addiction to alcohol or other drugs – maternal responsiveness reduced by mind-altering substances
- Young or inexperienced mother – lacks parenting skills

THE LESSONS OF ATTACHMENT HELP US HEAL

The powerful, life-altering lessons we learn from our attachment bond—our first love relationship—continue to teach us as adults. The gut-level knowledge we gained then guides us in understanding and improving our adult relationships and making them secure.

Adult relationships depend for their success on nonverbal forms of communication. Newborn infants cannot talk, reason, or plan; yet they are equipped to make sure their needs are met. Infants don't know what they need, they feel what they need, and communicate accordingly. When an infant communicates with a caretaker who understands and meets their physical and emotional needs, something wonderful occurs.

Relationships in which the parties are tuned in to each other's emotions are called attuned relationships, and attuned relationships teach us that:

- Nonverbal cues deeply impact our love relationships.

- Play helps us smooth over the rough spots in love relationships.

- Conflicts can build trust if we approach them without fear or a need to punish.

When we can recognize attitudes, assumptions, and behaviors as problems resulting from insecure attachment bonds, we can end their influence on our adult relationships. That recognition allows us to reconstruct the healthy nonverbal communication skills that produce an attuned attachment and successful relationships.

Intimate Relationships: pros vs cons

You can only attract someone to the level, or near it, that you reside on, because you now understand that you do not get what you want from life, but you get what you are. The key to any relationship is the "single state" because no matter how much you want a good relationship; it will never be better than you. You attract who you are, not what you want. So, focus on bettering you, and you will attract a better partner.

In my life-coaching relationships with clients, I have discovered a pattern of relationships and specifically, intimate relationships tend to be a large part of our overall conversations. Serving as a "sounding board", I try to place myself in the shoes of the other person, while having already walked a mile (and then some) in the returned citizen's shoes.

In one recent encounter with an ex-girlfriend of a recently returned citizen who served 30 years from the age of 16, she expressed her concern with "Tony", and his possible fraternizing "with the wrong girl". My response? "Every girl is the wrong girl... because Tony is not the "right" guy just yet." I went on further to explain that Tony must invest his time in becoming the best version of Tony, because, we get who we are and not what we want out of life.

What one fails to realize is that upon our release, we will be at a level of development, socially and emotionally, that it will be challenging to simply order from a menu, let alone get your license, enroll in school, find a job, find transportation without help from others. Thus, it is tempting to attach yourself to a significant other and in that attachment, you will develop a "caretaker" style of relationship where your partner is being fulfilled by helping you to get through the challenges you are facing.

The Problem: if you make the correct choices by growing through personal development then a year later, you will be able to do that which the "caretaker" relationship did for you and you will be facing a higher level of challenges that will attract a partner on that level. Your time must be used to invest in a stronger you and not in an intimate relationship. There are people and agencies that will guide you through the challenges that you will face. Being alone will be difficult but remember that you will never get the "right one" until you become the "right one". You need time...you need to especially be in a space where you dictate your time in a way that creates a better version of yourself daily, weekly, yearly, and forever because we embrace the law of harvest, which states that you will reap what you sow.

Relationship with Self: Know Thyself

The Greeks did many things correctly, first being, that they understood the most powerful path towards your purpose: Know Thy Self, written on the entrance to the Temple of Apollo at Delphi in Greece. Knowledge of Self is the path towards unlocking your greatness or the best version of yourself. The more you grow...the more you will realize that your personal and professional success will only come by way of looking in the mirror and not out the window. Your only power resides in the fact that you have a choice in how you will respond to what happens to you:

Stimulus (what happens to you) + Response (your power) = Circumstances

As you can see, when relying on physics and not philosophy, we gain the understanding that we are where we are because of how we have responded to the events around us. I could have easily chosen to read every book, do every assignment, and engross myself in television and sports instead of allowing my anger at my parents to push me towards a path of self-destruction that left victims in its path.

I lacked the emotional intelligence (a term we will study later in the book) to understand (under + stand, i.e., the truth I stand under) that my anger and pain for what my parents were struggling with was okay, but my response was not. For in choosing to disregard school and pursue drug dealing and armed robberies because I was angry at the world for dealing me a bad hand was to take a bad hand and make it worse.

The struggles of my childhood and adolescents could have made me stronger had I chosen different responses. We have a second, for some third, and for others fourth and more, chances to be successful in our reentry to the community. It's all in how we respond to the inevitable stress, conflict, and unfortunate drama that many of the people we left behind are still entrenched with. Many of us come from families and environments that use dysfunctional means of communicating and resolving conflict.

REMEMBER: we can only control how we respond and, in that knowledge and understanding resides our power to create our own circumstances, and our own destinies.

ANALYZE YOUR SKILLS

A successful job hunt begins by really knowing yourselves and what you enjoy doing.

Transferable Skills

Transferable skills are also referred to as "hire me" skills since every employer desires them. So named because they are skills that transfer from one type of work to another. Most adults have actually developed over 500 specific skills. Unfortunately, job seekers are only able to discuss 5-8 during an interview.

This section will help you identify your transferable skills which employers seek most. Being able to identify transferable skills will build confidence in the skills you possess, enhance your resume and application, and increase your effectiveness during the job interview process.

Objectives:

- Identify transferable skills and personal qualities that job seekers feel comfortable presenting to an employer.
- Provide written evidence of these skills and qualities in a form that could be presented directly to an employer.
- Learn to identify skills a job seeker can market to an employer.
- Identify specific occupations that utilize job seeker's transferable skills and personal qualities.

Overview:

Skills and abilities are the building blocks of job success. Learn to identify, demonstrate, and package with confidence the skills and personal qualities today's employers' desire.

The new economy requires workers who can transfer skills from one work setting to another, and who have the kinds of personal qualities that make organizations successful. Successful job seekers must know how to identify these skills and qualities within themselves and be able to describe and demonstrate them in ways that have meaning to employers. Participants in this section will learn how to identify and demonstrate a variety of skills and personal qualities desired by employers. They will be able to package their skills in a way that will communicate their desirability to employers.

TRANSFERABLE SKILLS AND CHARACTER TRAITS LIST

Based on your work experience, volunteer experience, military experience, educational experience and total life experience, place a check mark next to the skills that you possess. Next, circle skills and character traits that you believe are your strongest. Now list the words on a separate sheet of paper and write an example to show that you possess those skills. These will be your transferable skills you will want to feature on your application, resume, and in the interview responses.

Leadership	**Working With People**	**Dealing With Data**
Competitive	Aided	Analyze data
Decisive	Administer	Audit records
Delegate	Answered questions	Budgeting
Direct others	Attended/Assisted others	Calculate/compute
Explain things to others	Counsel others	Compile
Initiate new tasks	Demonstrate	Detail oriented
Make decisions	Instruct	Document research
Mediate problems	Listen	Evaluate
Motivate people	Negotiate	Investigate
Negotiate agreements	Patient	Keep financial records
Planning	Persuade	Locate information
Result-oriented	Supervise	Manage money
Take risks	Tactful	Posted
Conduct meetings	Teaching	Programmed
Self-confident	Tolerant	Proofread
Solve problems	Trusting	Record facts
Generate Ideas	Tutored	Take inventory
	Understanding	

Creative/Artistic

Artistic

Drawing

Expressive

Perform, act

Present artistic ideas

Using hands

Assemble things

Build things

Construct/repair buildings

Dismantled

Drive, operate vehicles

Fabricated

Loaded

Operating tools, machines

Repair things

Typed

Key Skills

Coordinated tasks

Instructing others

Implement

Managing resources

Managing people

Meeting deadlines

Serving the public

Negotiating

Organizing projects

Performed

Processed

Provided

Scheduled

Served

Supervised

Transported

Using Words

Articulate well

Communicate verbally

Correspond with others

Create new ideas

Design

Develop/create

Encouraged

Edit

Greeted

Justified

Presented

Promoted

Published

Speak publicly

Teamwork

Telephoned

Write clearly

DETERMINE YOUR WORK PREFERENCES

This exercise helps you to identify vocational interests, personal style, and work preferences. For example, your interests should be related to the jobs that you decide to pursue. Your values should not conflict with the occupation you choose. Complete this survey to identify your work preferences. Think about your work preferences and circle all the responses that best complete the phrase for you.

1.   I enjoy working with:
- ❑ data (information, words, numbers)
- ❑ people
- ❑ things (machines, equipment)

2.   I prefer working:
- ❑ indoors
- ❑ outdoors
- ❑ some inside and some outside

3.   I would like to work for a company:
- ❑ with less than 100 employees
- ❑ with 100 to 500 employees
- ❑ with 500 or more employees
- ❑ that is family owned

4.   I would like to work in a:
- ❑ large city
- ❑ medium city
- ❑ town or suburban area
- ❑ small town or rural area

5.   I want a job that requires:
   ❑ interacting with a lot of people
   ❑ some interaction with people
   ❑ very little human interaction
   ❑ no interaction with people

6.   I would like work duties that:
   ❑ frequently change
   ❑ vary from day to day
   ❑ are fairly routine
   ❑ never change

7.   I am willing to work overtime:
   ❑ as much as possible
   ❑ frequently
   ❑ occasionally
   ❑ never

8.   For the right job I am:
   ❑ eager to relocate
   ❑ willing to relocate
   ❑ not able to relocate
   ❑ not willing to relocate

9.   I prefer a job that involves:
   ❑ a lot of travel
   ❑ some travel
   ❑ no travel

10. I want to work
- ❏ full time
- ❏ part time
- ❏ temporary

11. List 5 things you like to do in your spare time.

____

____

____

____

12. What are your hobbies?

____

____

____

____

13. Are you more comfortable as a team member or a team leader?

____

____

____

____

14. Which of your past jobs did you like least? Why?

____

____

____

____

15. Which job did you like best? Why?

____

____

____

____

16. What kind of job would you do if you could choose any job?

____

____

____

____

17. What kind of training would you like to have, if any?

____

____

____

18. Why did you choose your previous field of work?

19. Take your responses and write your priority work preferences below.

Example: *I prefer a job where I: work with people, inside and outside, in a small city, and do some traveling. I am willing to relocate, but not out of state.*

THINGS TO REMEMBER FOR COMPLETING APPLICATIONS ON-SITE

- Take along a copy of information and dates that you might need to complete the application, rather than trying to remember them and making mistakes on the application.

- Remember that false information given on an application may be grounds for dismissal even after you have been employed for any length of time.

- Take "white-out" or an erasable pen, as well as a small dictionary, with you when completing applications.

FACE-TO-FACE CONTACTS

Creating a Good First Impression

People form an opinion of someone they meet in the first two to four minutes. For that reason, it is important that you pay attention to detail to create the best first impression you can. Some factors that affect the impression you make are appearance (hair, clothes, hygiene, jewelry, and make-up), movement, mannerisms, personal space, and speaking manner. A weak or too firm handshake makes a negative impression. You should practice shaking hands before an interview. To help enhance your chances of making a favorable impression, follow the basic rules discussed below.

Communicate Your Best Image in Appearance

Dress appropriately. Keep your dress understated, conservative, and neat. If you're unsure about what to wear, a good rule of thumb is to dress slightly better than you would to report to the job every day. For example, if blue jeans are acceptable attire at the workplace, you could wear casual dress pants to a job interview with such an organization. You can determine the dress code in a workplace by asking or observing, if it is a public place. If you are still unsure, a suit in a dark or neutral color is almost always a good choice. (Some social service agencies provide appropriate interview clothing to those in need.)

LEARN THE JOB MARKET

"How will I know where to look for work?"

"How will I know if the organization I'm interested in working for will be a good fit for me?"

Gain the instincts to feel where you may fit into a teamwork environment.

"I was looking for a job when I found this one. Why stop now, I know there are plenty of better jobs out there."

Objectives:

- Learn the importance of conducting labor market and employer research.
- Learn to use a variety of sources and tools to obtain labor market information.
- Learn how to conduct an informational interview.
- Learn to use labor market research resources.

Overview:

Before beginning an important journey, savvy travelers conduct research to "get a feel" for the area they will visit. Successful job seekers do the same thing. They know their skills and try to determine the type of workplace that uses these. This is called researching the labor market, which is the topic for this section.

Labor or job market research simply means getting a picture of the economy and workplace. Which businesses and other hiring organizations are in the area? What kind of work do they do? How do they hire? Which employers are most likely to be looking for someone like you? This section will help you answer these questions.

CAREER EXPLORATION

The closer the match between a job and your work preferences, financial needs, and transferable skills, the more likely you will be successful and happy in that job. Remember to search for the perfect job. But keep in mind, it is rare to find a perfect match in a job.
The following is a list of ways you can do career exploration:

- Library research

- Volunteer for an organization

- Employment Counseling

- Read business magazines

- Attend training or apprenticeship programs

- Talk to friends and relatives about their work and careers

- Network with people you get to meet

- Informational interviews

- Job shares

- Internships

- Job shadow

- Small Business Administration

- Employment agencies

- WorkSource Center

- Chamber of Commerce

- Better Business Bureau

Identify Specific Jobs

Now identify specific jobs you are interested in researching and pursuing.

Step 1: List 3 jobs that interest you and write the job titles below.

____

____

____

____

Step 2: Research the salary range and necessary qualifications and skills. Compare these to your financial needs, transferable skills, and education.

____

____

____

____

____

Step 3: Reality check yourself. Are the jobs you've identified available where you live? Are the jobs within a reasonable commute of one hour or less? For the jobs you want to get are you willing to relocate? Do you have the means and resources to move to where the jobs are available? Will the jobs pay for your cost-of-living, like housing, utilities, and transportation where you will live?

To overlook the above research can set an individual up for failure. The time and effort to study the labor market will pay off in numerous ways by setting realistic expectations, goals, planning and using your resources to your advantage.

RESEARCHING YOUR JOB MARKET

Successful job seekers take a focused approach to finding work: centered, narrow, strong. It is a planned approach that involves:

- Knowing your skills and what kinds of businesses use those skills.
- Studying employers.
- Using networking to contact employers.
- Contacting the person who does the hiring.
- Showing your skills to that employer, so that they know you can meet their needs.

Labor market study also lets you know what jobs are open in your area and where to find them.

- What are the jobs that you are skilled to do?
- Which employers hire people with your skills and abilities?
- What needs do the employers have in your area that you could fill?
- How do these employers hire?

Finding the answers to these questions will make time you put into your job search much more useful.

Begin the research trail: There are many resources that give company listings and facts about them. Use these lists to find out what is taking place in your desired line of work, as well as facts about employers. You can also use these lists to find employers you want to contact for job openings or to find out more about their business.

Useful resources:

- ***WorkSource Centers*** – will have a wealth of local job market information, who major employers are, new employers to the area, and access to resources for in-depth research of other labor markets statewide. Ask to learn and use the WorkForce Explorer Internet site.

- ***Local phone books*** - especially yellow pages and business section, and blue pages.
- ***The Chamber of Commerce and Economic Development Council*** - has listings that describe member business in the area.
- ***The local library*** - contains resources including:
  - ***Local Union & Trade Organizations***
  - ***Local business Journals*** and report on businesses in the area
  - ***Lead Source Directories*** list of local businesses by zip code.
  - ***Dunn & Bradstreet*** lists of manufacturers, corporate management, and transportation companies (also available on the Internet).
- ***The Internet*** job boards and individual company web pages.

WHAT EMPLOYERS LOOK FOR WHEN HIRING

Employers ranked these factors that they consider in making hiring decisions and what they consider most important.

Attitude ---46%
Communication Skills --42%
Previous Work Experience--40%
Recommendations from Current Employees ---------------------------------------34%
Previous Employer Recommendations ---34%
Industry-based Credentials --32%
(Verifying Applicant's Skill) Years of Completed Schooling ---------------------------29%
Scores on Test Administered as Part of the Interview-----------------------------------25%
Academic Performance---25%
Experience or Reputation of Applicant's School --24%
Teacher Recommendations ---21%
(Source: U.S. Census Bureau National Survey)

QUALITIES EMPLOYERS WANT

Today's employers want workers whose job skills and work attitude will help the workplace succeed. Most employers want and expect certain qualities. In the spaces provided below, describe what each quality would look like on a given job.

Attitude	
Communication	
Teamwork	
Dependability	
Self-Motivated	
Flexible	
Problem Solver	

SUCCESSFUL PEOPLE VS. UNSUCCESSFUL PEOPLE

Successful People	Unsuccessful People
Expect success Romans 8:28 And we know that all things work together for good to them that love God, to them who are the called according to his purpose.	**Expect Failure**
Think they can Philippians 4:13 I can do all things through Christ who strengthens me.	**Don't want to try**
Try whole heartedly Ephesians 6:6 Not with eyeservice, as men pleasers; but as the servants of Christ, doing the will of God from the heart	**Try half heartedly**
Fake it till they make it 2 Corinthians 5:7 For we walk by faith, not by sight.	**Blame others for their lack of success**
Take responsibility for success and mistakes Romans 12:2 And be not conformed to this world: but be ye transformed by the renewing of your mind, that ye may prove what is that good, and acceptable, and perfect, will of God.	**Deny any responsibility**
Take action Matthew 6:33 But seek ye first the kingdom of God, and his righteousness; and all these things shall be added unto you.	**Give up**
Have patience 1 Corinthians 13:4-5 Charity suffered long, and is kind; charity envied not; charity vaunted not itself, is not puffed up, [5]Doth not behave itself unseemly, seek not her own, is not easily provoked, thinketh no evil.	**Have no discipline**

The difference between success and failure is a choice. It's much easier to give up than to do what it takes to achieve. The time, energy and effort to accomplish add value to anything meaningful in life.

PREPARATION MAKES PERMANENT

- **Arrive early.** Plan your schedule and route so you arrive 10-15 minutes prior to the appointment. Allow time to stop in the building's bathroom, if there is a public one, for a last-minute check on your appearance.

- **Bring a black pen,** extra copies of your resume, your reference list, copies of licenses, driving record (for jobs requiring it), and social security or alien card.

- **Bring any other documentation** supporting your qualifications (portfolio, work samples, references, etc.).

- **Introduce yourself politely** using your first and last name and stating the first and last name of the individual you are to see.

- **Do not chew gum.**

- **Do not smoke.** It is best not to smoke just before an interview as many people find the smell on your clothes and hair offensive.

- **Say, "It's nice to meet you"** in your initial greeting to the interviewer. Shake hands firmly.

- **Address the interviewer as Mr.__________ or Ms. ____________** unless you are requested to do otherwise. Don't assume that if the interviewer calls you by your first name you are both on a first-name basis!

- **Be willing to make a bit of small talk,** possibly about the weather, about the interviewer's good directions, or about traffic on the way to the interview.

- **Speak clearly,** and in a positive, audible manner – but don't be too loud.

TELEPHONE INTERVIEW
"DO'S AND DON'TS"

DOs

- ✓ Answer the telephone professionally (If it is prearranged, YOU should answer)
- ✓ Find a quiet place
- ✓ Comfortable place to sit
- ✓ Table to lay out your portfolio and papers. (You need to be able to easily go through your notes, take notes and concentrate)
- ✓ Dress for the interview
- ✓ Speak slowly, take your time, and enunciate
- ✓ Turn cell phone and call-waiting off
- ✓ Give short and concise responses

DON'Ts

- ✘ DO NOT take calls at work
- ✘ DO NOT use a cell phone (unless absolutely necessary). Inform the interviewer
- ✘ DO NOT walk around while talking
- ✘ DO NOT slump down in your chair. It can cause breathlessness and takes away from the authority of your voice.
- ✘ DO NOT take the interview while driving
- ✘ DO NOT take the call in the presence of others (you should be alone)
- ✘ DO NOT chew gum, drink, or eat during the interview

REASON FOR LEAVING LAST EMPLOYER

When listing your reasons for leaving, do not say that you were fired, quit, or that you were arrested and taken away. Below are examples of reasons for leaving that do not raise red flags of concern.

- Personal (now resolved)
- Will explain at interview
- Laid off or reduction in force
- Relocated
- Job ended
- Seasonal position
- Transportation issue (now resolved)
- Lack of hours/work
- Career Change
- Promoted
- Took time off to care for an ill family member
- Family reasons (now resolved)

Be sure to use the reason that fits your unique circumstance. Remember, you must still be prepared to provide an explanation when asked in an interview.

LIST OF JOB RESOURCES

Here is a short list of companies that hire felons depending on their record. Many other companies do hire regardless of records so check their websites for possible matches.

Federal Bonding Program:
https://www.flgov.com/wp-content/uploads/childadvocacy/Federal_Bonding_Program_Questions-EOG_(002).pdf

Transportation:
Swift Transportation (https://www.swifttrans.com/)
C.R. England (https://www.crengland.com/)
U.P.S. (https://www.ups.com/us/en/Home.page)
Cardinal Logistics (https://www.cardlog.com/)

Grocery:
Win Co Foods (https://www.wincofoods.com/)
Trader Joe's (https://www.traderjoes.com/home)
Publix (https://www.publix.com/)
Kroger (https://www.kroger.com/)
Safeway (https://www.safeway.com/)
Whole Foods (https://www.wholefoodsmarket.com/)

Retail:
WalMart (https://www.walmart.com/)
Target (https://www.target.com/)

Hospitality:
Marriott (https://careers.marriott.com/)
Wyndham (https://careers.wyndhamhotels.com/)
Hilton (https://jobs.hilton.com/us/en)
Hyatt (https://jobs.hilton.com/us/en)

Restaurants:
Applebee's (https://www.applebees.com/en)
Chik-fil-a (https://www.chick-fil-a.com/)
Maggiano's (http://www.maggianosjobs.com/)

Packaging:
Aramark (https://www.aramark.com/)
General Mills (https://www.generalmills.com/)

Manufacturing:
Ford (https://corporate.ford.com/careers.html)
Microsoft (https://careers.microsoft.com/us/en)
Stanley Black and Decker (https://www.stanleyblackanddecker.com/careers/working-here)

Chapter 5 – Child Support, Family Reunification, & Ways Family & Friends Can Assist

CHILD SUPPORT AND INCARCERATION

There are two primary ways by which noncustodial parents with child support orders may intersect with the criminal justice system. On one path, the noncustodial parent is not in compliance with a child support obligation and that noncompliance may lead to incarceration (short-term, primarily in local jails) as a result of either a civil contempt or criminal non-support action taken by the state. The other way is for noncustodial parents who are incarcerated for a criminal offense and have a current or delinquent child support obligation. The incarceration is not related to child support and they may be incarcerated for longer periods of time in a state or federal prison. While child support isn't the reason for incarceration for these parents, the ongoing child support obligation has repercussions for their confinement, release and re-entry.

As of Dec. 31, 2017 there were approximately 1.49 million people in federal and state prison. More than 50 percent of those inmates have one or more child under the age of 18, leaving an estimated 2.7

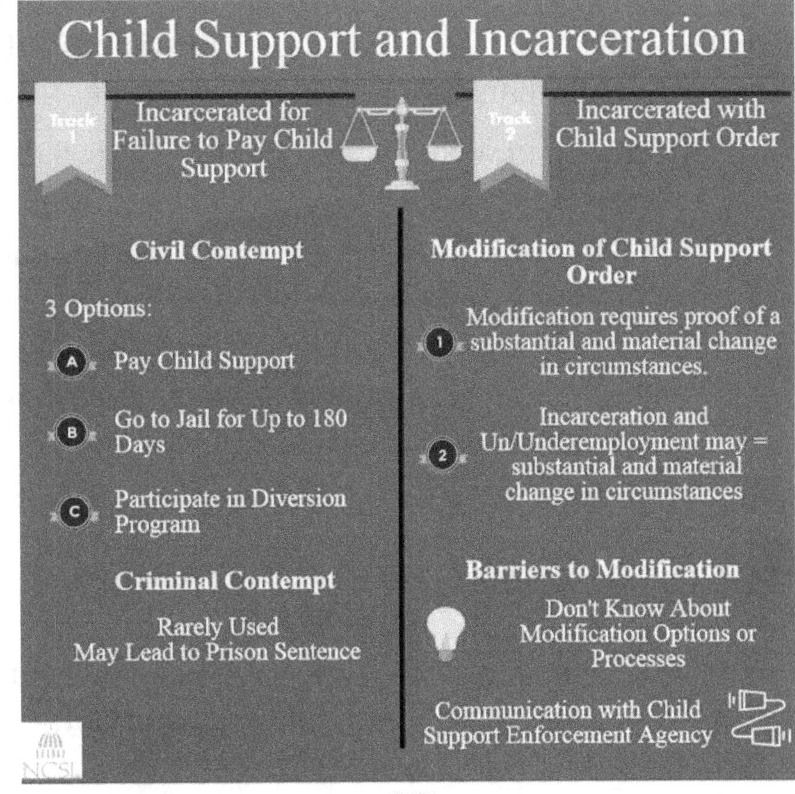

million children with a parent incarcerated. In addition, a 2003 study estimated that one quarter of inmates in prisons had a child support case. Based on current prison populations, this suggests that approximately 400,000 inmates have a child support case.

The distinction between those noncustodial parents who are incarcerated for failure to pay child support and those who are incarcerated for a separate criminal offense who also have child support orders is an important one. The available approaches to improving child support compliance and encouraging ongoing, consistent child support payments within these populations are very different, particularly considering the reasons for and potential length of the incarceration. Below is a further discussion address the needs of incarcerated noncustodial parents.

New Federal Rule on Child Support

On Dec. 20, 2016, the Office of Child Support Enforcement (OCSE) published final rules updating the rules regarding child support enforcement. The rule is intended to increase the effectiveness of the child support program for all families and provide for more flexibility in state child support programs.

The rule specifically addresses incarcerated noncustodial parents and incarceration for failure to pay child support, as well as modification procedures for incarcerated noncustodial parents. The major provisions of the rule regarding incarcerated noncustodial parents are:

- Incarcerated with a Child Support Order: the rule ensures the right of all parents to seek a review of their order when their circumstances change. While these provisions apply to all parties involved, they specifically address incarcerated noncustodial parents and their ability to have the child support order reviewed and potentially modified while they are incarcerated. The rule prohibits states from treating incarceration as voluntary unemployment for purposes of modifying a child support order. Currently 36 states and D.C. treat incarceration as involuntary unemployment.

Incarcerated with Child Support Order

On average, an incarcerated parent with a child support order has the potential to leave prison with nearly $20,000 in child support debt, having entered the system with around half that amount owed.

According to 2013 data from the Bureau of Justice:

- 46 percent of incarcerated parents have high school diploma or equivalent, as compared to 82% of men ages 18-34.

- Nearly 60 percent of black men who are high school dropouts have done time by their mid-30s.

- About two-thirds of people in prison or jail were employed at least part time before arrest with a median income of less than $1000 per month.

Modification During Incarceration

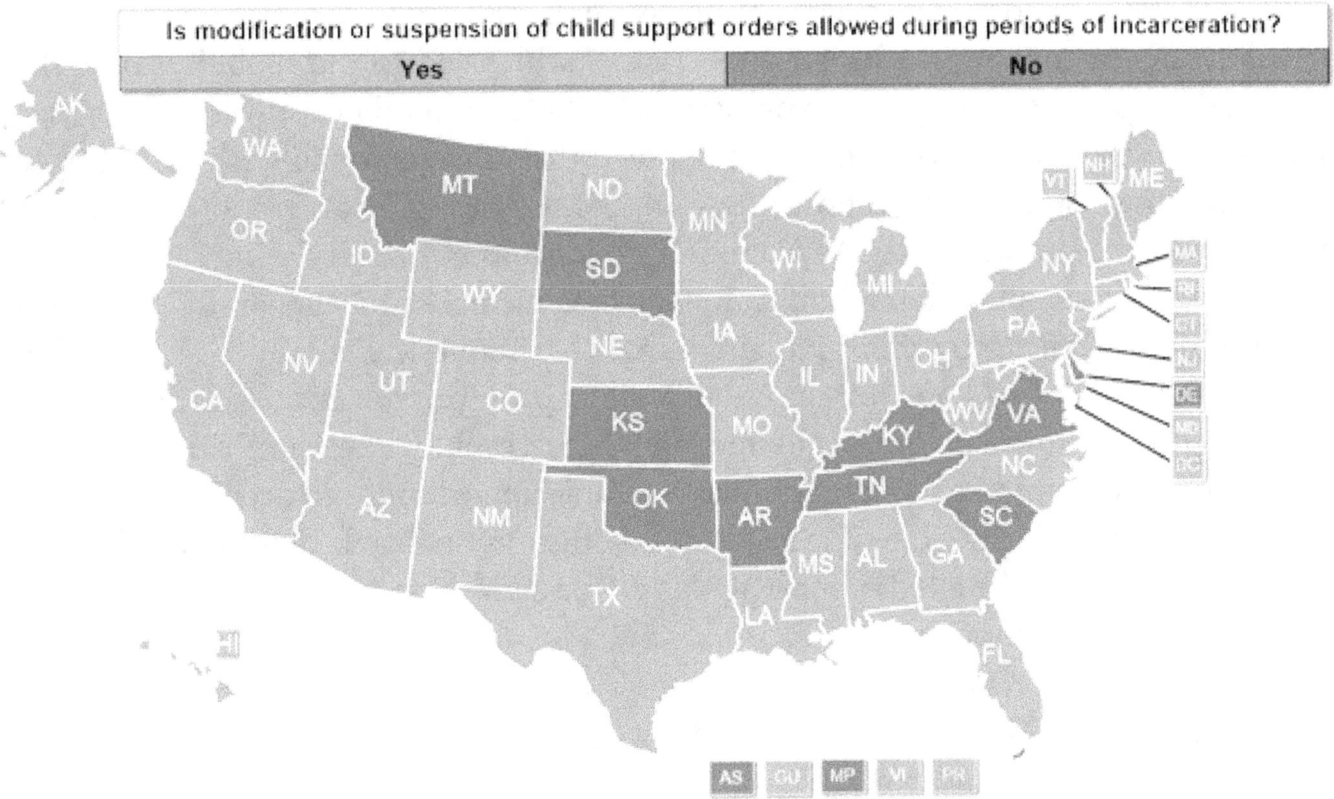

Whether a parent is incarcerated or not, a material and substantial change in circumstances is required to modify child support orders in the majority of jurisdictions. Two situations that may be treated as a material and substantial change in circumstances are incarceration and unemployment.

Some states allow incarceration to be considered a substantial change in circumstances allowing for modification while others do not allow incarceration alone to be a sufficient reason for modification and would require other circumstances to be shown in order to modify. State policies regarding modification of child support during incarceration vary and depend on a number of factors.

A significant reduction in income due to a job loss or job change is generally considered a material and substantial change for purposes of modifying child support, as long as the job loss or reduction in earnings was involuntary. Conversely, voluntary un- or underemployment in order to avoid payment of child support is not considered to be a material and substantial change of circumstances and therefore does not warrant consideration for modifying child support.

Approximately 40 states and D.C. currently treat imprisonment as involuntary unemployment which means the obligor could request a modification. Certain exceptions to this determination exist if the reason for the incarceration is related to the failure to pay child support or avoidance of child support. A small number of states treat incarceration as voluntary unemployment because the crime, which led to the inability to work or pay child support, is considered a voluntary act. As such, modification of child support during incarceration is not allowed in those states. The new federal rule, discussed above, prohibits state child support programs from treating incarceration as voluntary unemployment, allowing for modification of child support orders during incarceration.

The states that allow for modification during incarceration generally require the noncustodial parent to be proactive in making that request. This process requires the incarcerated parent to know of the modification procedure and access the necessary resources in order to obtain timely modification. Most recently, however, California passed legislation which requires the suspension of a child support order to occur automatically when an obligor is incarcerated or involuntarily institutionalized. In addition, Vermont and Wisconsin allow the child support agency to file a motion to modify the child support orders of incarcerated obligors.

RESOURCE SOURCE

The federal Office of Child Support Enforcement has a State by State How to Change a Child Support Order page to inform child support obligors and state policymakers on the available resources and processes involved.

SUBSTANCE ABUSE

Drug abuse threatens to disrupt even the most stable of lives. It creates mental, physical, and emotional turmoil that can, even for a well-adjusted person, be exceedingly difficult to overcome. For those who are in or have spent a significant amount of time within prison, balance is elusive, and during their tenure of incarceration, they may in fact develop greater instability that can provoke a previous addiction or incite circumstances that cause an individual to start abusing substances for the first time.

What Is Post Incarceration Syndrome?

Post Incarceration Syndrome (PICS) is a mental disorder that occurs in individuals either currently incarcerated or recently released; symptoms are found to be most severe for those who encountered extended periods of solitary confinement and institutional abuse. These symptoms stem from an individual encountering an environment of punishment that provided little opportunity for education, vocational training, or rehabilitation. There are several facets of this disorder as follows:

- ***Institutionalized Personality Traits:*** This passivity is derived from an individual's ongoing state of learned helplessness, as they encounter various deprivations within their incarceration. This suppression of their personal nature and individualized critical thinking rises as a defense against prison authorities and also towards their fellow inmates, who at times may challenge their safety.

- ***Post-Traumatic Stress Disorder (PTSD):*** This disorder is based on trauma originating both prior to and during their time in prison; individuals may suffer from cognitive impairment, feel "on edge," develop periodic angry outbursts, they may mentally relive events, and have distorted or negative feelings about themselves or others.

- ***Antisocial Personality Traits (ASPT):*** These passive-aggressive tendencies are a coping mechanism against the abuse derived within the prison system and also in response to their fellow inmates' predatory and abusive behaviors; it can result in an individual becoming antagonistic towards both authority and their peers.

- ***Social-Sensory Deprivation Syndrome:*** This is caused from prolonged periods of solitary confinement that deprive an individual of any social contact and inflicts a state of sensory deprivation upon them.

- ***Substance Abuse Disorders:*** Inmates, both current and former, often turn to drugs to self-medicate as a way to temper and escape the symptoms and disorders caused by PICS.

The extent in which these symptoms manifest is based on several factors including: the foundation of coping skills they had prior to being incarcerated, the length of their sentence, the frequency and intensity of the abuse they endured, the amount and length of time spent in solitary confinement, and the extent to which they were able to participate in institutional programs.

BECOMING AT-RISK FOR PICS WHILE IN PRISON

It is becoming increasingly evident that many inmates haven't been imparted with the social skills that are necessary for reintroduction into civilian life, whether it be from their own apathy or more commonly, the lack of accessibility within the system. The following areas, though crucial to their success and development, are commonly lacking.

Education:

Sadly, within the correctional education system that's prevalent within the prison system today, there is a notable deficiency in the teaching of both vocational and rehabilitative skills that may transcend the bounds of prison life and be applicable in the outside world.

The Legislative Analyst's Office of California cites that they "found low student enrollment levels compared to the number of inmates who could benefit from these programs, inadequate participation rates by inmates, a flawed funding allocation methodology, ineffective case management, and lack of regular program evaluation." While these findings are specific to California, these are common issues within our nation's correctional education system as a whole.

This misappropriation creates a divide between what is needed for the individual to succeed and survive and what skills they actually possess to take care of themselves. Thus, many turn again (or for the first time) to the drug world, either within or after their incarceration. The LAO also stated that "inmates are less likely to engage in disruptive and violent incidents when they are actively engaged in a program instead of being idle." Thus, inmates have a reduced risk of developing PICS and a greater chance towards obtaining stability upon their release. A study authored by the Correctional Education Association for the Department of Education found that inmates who took part in classes, whether they be vocational or at high school or college level, had a reduced rate of recidivism within three years of being released.

Vocational:

There are a variety of programs within the system that allow for an individual to work during their sentence; however, these skills often do not easily transcend the bounds between prison and life afterward. Additionally, it can be difficult for individuals that were incarcerated to find work—inmates need to have greater access to learning marketable skills and those that revolve around job-searching and the interview process. A RAND Cooperation report found that inmates "were 28 percent more likely to be employed after release from prison than [those] who did not receive such training."

As an individual struggles to find gainful employment, they may get disconcerted on two levels: first, financially, and second, as they struggle to find the confidence and fulfillment the responsibility of a job can impart. This struggle may unfortunately encourage some individuals to turn to the drug world as a means to achieve financial solubility or to ease their emotional duress. This puts them at greater risk for returning to prison and for also developing a substance abuse problem.

Rehabilitation:

Inmates can be at a huge disadvantage when they return to society or their families; most inmates struggled prior to their incarceration and their time spent fulfilling their sentence may have served to further create a rift, leaving them inept at contending with real-world situations and stressors. Unfortunately, as they lack the necessary social skills and emotional rehabilitation to transition back to a civilian life, many inmates seek solace in drugs, choosing to self-medicate their feelings of loneliness, anger, depression, and anxiety.

In all likelihood, many individuals have never been granted proper rehabilitation or education to address the complexities of a substance abuse disorder, nor the appropriate measures and tools that are necessary to contend with the pursuit and upkeep of their recovery. Instead, they may still mentally and emotionally attribute drugs to other things, most notably camaraderie, structure, and a source of income. Rehabilitation treatment and programs can, as cited by the Federal Bureau of Prisons (BOP):

- Reduce relapse, criminality, recidivism, and inmate misconduct
- Increase the level of the offender's stake in societal norms, levels of education and employment upon return to the community
- Improve health and mental health symptoms and conditions, as well as relationships

How does PICS Create a Greater Health Risk for Substance Abuse?

In prison populations, inmates often enter the system with a reduced level of coping skills due to their way of life; some may already suffer PTSD or have emotional or mental health issues. As the individual contends with the restrictive nature of their incarceration, violent episodes or abuse by their peers and even prison staff, their mental health falters leaving them at greater risk for substance abuse. The National Institute on Drug Abuse states that, "Among individuals with substance use disorders, 30 to 60 percent meet the criteria for comorbid PTSD."

As those in the prison population seek to survive within a severe and punitive environment, they build off preexisting symptoms and develop both institutionalized and anti-social personality traits. In an environment where one must be passive in the face of authority and commonly aggressive to their fellow inmates, they suppress their critical and individual thinking, emotional responses, and personal expression.

Thus, when faced with the reality of a substance abuse disorder, they are severely limited in their ability to comprehend some of the crucial insights and practices that are needed for recovery, such as honesty, humility, self-awareness, and self-care. Without proper support, education, and the investment and care of a dedicated staff, it can become increasingly difficult to learn about these things and commit them to practice

Action Plan

Contending with PICS will in fact make your recovery more intense, however it is not unattainable. It is crucial that those who suffer from PICS, PTSD, and substance abuse problems seek the support from physicians and staff that are trained in these areas; these individuals can help you develop coping skills and methods to reduce your risk for substance abuse and recidivism. If you do find yourself struggling with substance abuse after your release, entering into a recovery facility can help acclimate you to the tools, education, and confidence you need to succeed in finding wellness.

GIVING BACK TO THE COMMUNITY WE TOOK SO MUCH FROM

Many program managers work with their community partners to find new volunteer opportunities, supporting the community and empowering participants. Community service gives participants a sense of belonging and a feeling of personal investment in where they live. It can also give individuals a greater sense of pride in their reentry process, as it can create a feeling of making amends to the community. Volunteering and giving back to the community give those who have returned from prison a sense of belonging and is a great step towards becoming a positive force in the world. Additionally, no organizations have unlimited resources so the time and energy our participants and staff volunteer are always greatly appreciated and allows these community resources to have an even greater impact.

Lastly, staying in motion allows for the unforeseeable opportunities that result from giving and becoming and, as such, so shall you receive. I have worked my way into many employment opportunities by simply volunteering my service and time. For me, giving back to the very community that I harmed reinforces the values and habits needed to not only remain free but also to succeed both professionally and personally.

RETURNING HOME – THE FAMILY STRUCTURE

Families of the incarcerated look forward to the release date but reunification isn't always smooth and easy. In this chapter, we discuss the challenges spouses face when husbands are released and provide tips to overcome them. Two factors contribute to the challenges the spouse faces. One is, difficult past experiences with her husband, and the other is her expanded role in the family during his incarceration. To reunite successfully, the couple should understand that things have changed and they themselves are now different people. Their family too has changed as children grow older. Husband and wife will have to renegotiate their roles in the family and if they are not on the same page, reunification may not be successful. Note that the one incarcerated can be either the man or the woman. For simplicity, we denote the man (husband) as in prison and the woman (wife) as being at home.

CHALLENGES

Communication: While he is in prison, the couple will need to work together to maintain their relationship as a couple. Staying in communication will be a challenge for both, but especially for the wife who now has more on her plate.

Wife's role is now bigger: With her husband away, the wife has to care for her children and their home, in most cases, alone. She needs to make decisions without the support of her partner. Mom also is now the sole person responsible for the preservation, strengthening and ultimate growth of the family. She is taking on a lot and this makes her a stronger mother and braver person in general.

Husband's role is now less: In prison, her husband is in a new environment with different rules and its own challenges. He is no longer providing for the physical needs of his family and can no longer provide emotional support in the way he was used to.

Preparing for Reunification

Reunification as a goal: Preparing for reunification should start from the time of incarceration. If possible, the couple should agree to work towards reunification. This helps them to look to the future. It would lessen the pain of separation, even if incarceration is lengthy.

Keeping the family together: Incarceration can be stressful for the children and mom maintains the family while the father is incarcerated, by nurturing the mental and emotional health of the children.

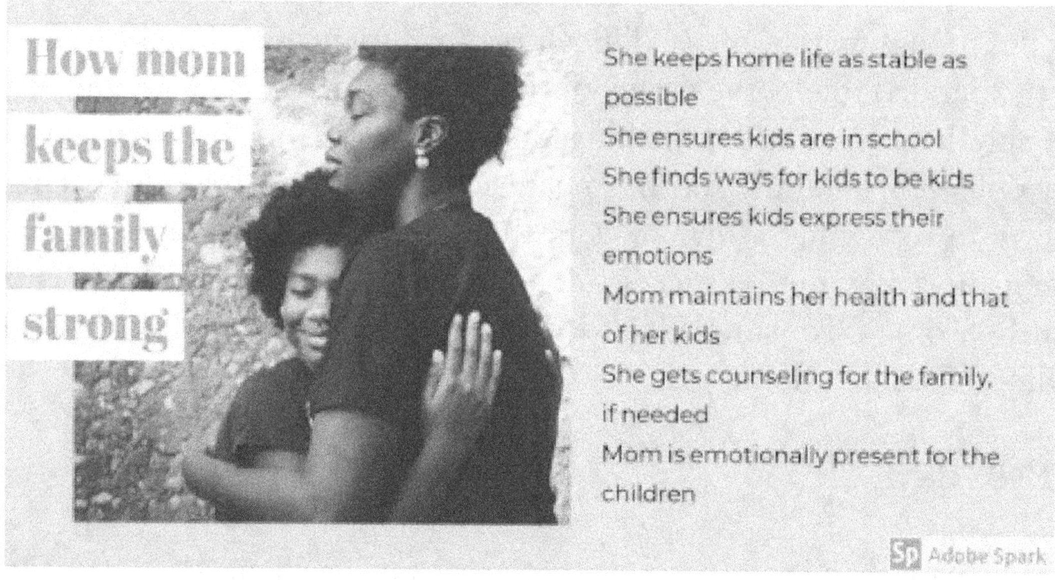

HOW MOM KEEPS THE FAMILY STRONG

When dad returns, the entire family can focus on reunifying as the family has persevered and grown positively. If she is successful in keeping the family strong, the issues that may occur at reunification will be less.

AFTER THE HUSBAND'S RETURN

Practice patience and listen: The couple should remember their experiences during the husband's incarceration were very different. Patience is needed to learn what each other went through and it may be very difficult to talk through the experiences.

Communicate: As a couple, they may need to relearn how to communicate. Carving out time to reconnect away from family and friends after he comes home to give yourselves time to reunite.

Manage expectations: Both husband and wife may have different expectations of what happens after reunification as life is now different. Before reunification, counseling is helpful to prepare the couple and the family. Having conversations about the future helps to manage expectations.

Take time to adjust: The husband will need time to adjust to life outside of prison. It might be very different on the outside depending on the length of incarceration. Kids will be older and they are going to need special time to reconnect with their dad.

Renegotiate roles: For the wife, the change of role after reunification may be the biggest challenge. Her responsibilities when her husband comes home will change because now it will be a shared partnership once again. More importantly, her husband will be relearning his role in the family and compromises will be key as the couple readjusts to being a family unit.

WHEN REUNIFICATION ISN'T DESIRABLE?

Some families completely sever contacts with the incarcerated person for reasons like moral issues around incarceration or domestic abuse. Reunification is sometimes undesirable, but the father may have the right to a relationship with his children.

"FRIENDS" – PEER PRESSURE VS. PEER INFLUENCE

Though both terms, peer pressure and peer influence, look similar at a glance, there is a difference between them. In a workplace, a peer is someone at a similar level such as same grade, same gender, status, etc. Positive peer interactions and relationships help organizations in many ways. The two terms associated with workplace peers are peer pressure and peer influence. The key difference between peer pressure and peer influence is that peer pressure is the pressure from one's peers to act in a way that is acceptable to the others in the same group. This can be a positive pressure or a negative pressure. Peer influence is when a peer's act influences the others also to act in the same way. Peer pressure is a forcible action and peer influence is a persuading/influencing action.

WHAT IS PEER PRESSURE?

Peer pressure is the pressure from one's peers to act in a way that is acceptable to the others in the same group. Peer pressure is a forcible action. This can be a positive pressure or a negative pressure. When facing reentry, you will be faced with challenges that are unfamiliar which will lead you to being tempted to pursue the familiar, or old associations, old ways of making money, and old hangouts. Understanding that your environment will determine whether you successfully reintegrate means that you will need to plan before your release, and post release, for the natural inclination to revert back to comfortable peers, places, and processes. The key is to remember that growth is uncomfortable, so don't look comfort but endure the process of growth which means discomfort.

SEVEN WAYS TO HELP YOUR LOVED ONE ADJUST TO LIFE AFTER PRISON

Today's the day—your loved one is coming home! You and your family are excited. Now everything can go back to normal, right? The truth is, your loved one is going to have to adjust to life on the outside. They will most likely have to deal with culture shock, depression, and anger. In addition, they will also have challenges with the social stigma and the collateral consequences that come with a criminal record. How can you help your loved one adjust to life after prison? Here are seven ways to consider.

1. UNDERSTAND CULTURE SHOCK

Depending on the length of your loved one's sentence, one of the greatest challenges to reentry may be culture shock. The longer they were in prison, the greater the culture shock may be.

Your loved one will notice new technology, the rise of social media for communication, newer versions of cell phones or cell phones in general, and new language that has been introduced since they were last out of prison. They will need your help to adjust to their new "normal."

The key to helping your loved one with culture shock is to be patient and show them your and God's love. Offer them help with decision making, new cultural norms, and life organization.

WHAT IS CULTURE SHOCK?

Culture shock is the disorienting feeling a person can get when they suddenly have to adapt to an unfamiliar culture or way of life. It can also occur when a person returns after a long period of absence to his or her former culture. This is sometimes called "reverse culture shock."

2. BE AWARE OF DEPRESSION

Depression after incarceration is very common. Readjusting to daily life is challenging and working towards finding a job with a criminal record and gaining financial stability can be frustrating. If therapy is not an option, there are other steps you and your loved one can take to improve their mental health and happiness.

SET SMALL GOALS

Start with one goal a day. Encourage them to reward themselves with something small, like take a long walk or enjoy a special meal, when each goal is achieved. The more success they have, regardless of how small, the more confident and happier they will be.

WORK WITH YOUR LOVED ONE ON THEIR SELF-TALK

For example, if you're loved one is prone to think, "I can't get a job. I am a failure," encourage them to tell themselves something like, "I haven't gotten a job *yet*. If I keep applying to jobs, I will eventually get one." Reaffirming positive thinking and connecting with others who think positively will eventually change the way your loved one sees the world around them.

If improvement is slow or nonexistent, consider reaching out to a therapist or other professional for additional help.

3. COMMUNICATE YOUR FRUSTRATION

Frustration for both you and your loved one is expected at this stage of your relationship. Your loved one may face frustration in their adjustment to living in a home, troubles with vulnerability, their employment search, treatment, and culture shock. You will also face frustration with the changes that occurred during their incarceration. Many times, they may not leave incarceration the same person you envisioned.

The best way to improve feelings of frustration is through communication. Talk to each other about how you perceive the way they express their frustration and decide the best way to express these feelings. Finding a middle ground and keeping accountability will keep the dialogue open to improve your communication.

4. MANAGE ANGER

In prison, aggression and anger are methods of protection. Outside prison culture, these displays are not as acceptable. Your loved one will need to find a way to control this anger and channel it into productivity.

Whenever they feel angry, encourage your loved one to take a step back and focus on slow breathing for 10 seconds. Then try to discuss and isolate the cause of their anger.

Lastly, try to understand what they hoped to achieve with their anger and how they can achieve it in a more effective and controlled way.

5. DEAL WITH REJECTION

Rejection will come in many forms during your loved one's first months at home. Employers, former friends, and even some family, may reject them due to the stigma they associate with incarceration. You will need to help them learn how to accept the rejection, move on, and continue to improve themselves and their circumstances.

Remind them to be easy on themselves. They are not a failure. They must keep working, stay focused, and give themselves credit for the progress they have made. Encourage them to focus on their ultimate desired outcome rather than their past failures.

6. RESIST NEGATIVE INFLUENCES

There is always external pressure to conform to the group to gain acceptance. If your loved one's friends and family are pushing them to improve, work hard, and take time to connect with God and other followers of Christ, they will find that they will want to do the same.

Otherwise, the best way to resist negative influences is to be aware of them. Discuss your loved one's individual restraints, comfort levels, and what they believe is right and wrong and encourage them to stick to these restraints in all scenarios. It is important for your loved one to understand their own individual needs and goals before going into more group settings.

7. COMBAT ADDICTION

Your loved one may have developed an addiction before or during their prison sentence. When released, they may not be the same person you expected them to be.

Addictions are incredibly difficult to work through without support. Your loved one will need your emotional support, love, care, and guidance to help them. Many times, they may need help from a licensed therapist or doctor to provide a clear, research-backed path to beating their addiction. Ultimately, it is your love and support that will guide them through the process of healing.

Eight Ways To Prepare For A Loved One's Reentry

Preparing you and your family for the return of your incarcerated loved one can be beneficial to your loved one's reentry…and your family's adjustment. Here are eight ways to prepare for a loved one's reentry.

1. Understand Their Probation And Parole

When your loved one is released from prison, they will most likely have conditions of parole. Some of these conditions may include: curfew, geographic limits, mandatory job search, drug or alcohol tests, community treatment center attendance, electronic monitoring, and many other possibilities.

If possible, the best way to help your loved one comply with their restrictions is to develop a relationship with their probation officer and ensure that you are knowledgeable concerning the details of their parole. This will ensure that both you and your loved one are aware of all conditions of release and will minimize the chance of a parole violation as a result of miscommunication.

2. Save Money

When your loved one comes home, they will need some time to get back on their feet. It will take time to readjust to the culture outside prison, relearn how to schedule their time, and find a job. During this process, they will most likely need financial support for their food, clothes, and housing.

If you are able to support your loved one, make it clear that your financial support is short term and conditional on their efforts to find a job and become financially independent.

3. PLAN FOR YOUR RELATIONSHIP

The days before your loved one is released are exciting. You are envisioning your lives as they had been in the past and looking forward to finally spending time with your loved one again. But after the first few days or weeks, challenges will arise.

You will need a plan for when the initial excitement wears off. Both you and your loved one should have an in-person conversation about what your relationship will look like after the excitement, including your physical and emotional boundaries.

Develop a plan for the hard days, the employment search, and the best way to address your children's potential reactions.

For your loved one, building family relationships and developing ties to the community are key in making sure that he or she does not put themselves in a situation that may lead back to prison. By looking ahead and planning for the various emotional stages of their reentry, you will both be better prepared to face the challenges.

4. LOOK AHEAD TO FUTURE NEEDS

Before your loved one's release, consider finding resources that you or your family may need in the future. Even if you do not believe that you will need them now, it is better to be prepared for the unexpected.

There are nonprofits and other organizations that provide resources for financial support, food, and shelter. In addition, you can also find resources for clothing, transportation, and health care.

Be sure to keep an eye out for family therapy and individual mental health support.

Finding employment assistance, education, and training services will help when your loved one begins to look for a job.

5. FIND POTENTIAL RESOURCE SUPPORT AGENCIES

Your family will need to readjust to your loved one being home and the potential behavioral changes resulting from incarceration.

Church and support groups with other like-minded individuals will provide a source of friendship, stability, trust, and advice for when

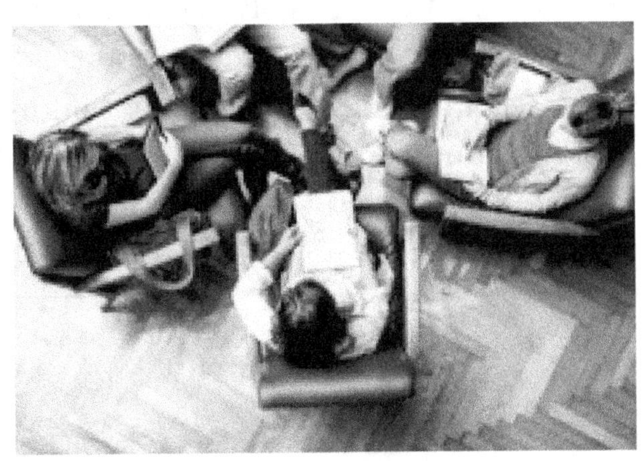

the times get tough. Having a larger network of friends will help each person in your family get through the tough times together. Some examples of resources centers are Salvation Army, food banks, shelters, Catholic charities, and churches that are funded to provide food banks. In the beginning months of reintegration these will be great sources of support and it is imperative that you not only accept that help but reach out for that help because it is said, *a closed mouth doesn't get fed.*

6. GET READY FOR YOUR LOVED ONE'S JOB SEARCH

Your loved one's job search may be one of the most challenging parts of reentry. Many companies are wary about hiring individuals with a criminal record, which will make your loved one's job search more challenging.

Before they are released, consider researching groups that assist former prisoners with their job search. Look for companies that have "banned the box" and stated that they are proponents of second chances and are willing to hire individuals with a criminal history.

Furthermore, because your loved one's job search is going to be challenging, you must prepare for the emotional strain of the search as well. Your loved one will likely have feelings of frustration and anger. Prepare for this and remind your loved one that all it takes is one successful interview.

7. TALK TO YOUR CHILDREN

Before your loved one returns home, you will need to prepare your children. Just like when your husband or wife was initially incarcerated, your kids will need time to adjust to the sudden change in family dynamic and home life. They may be angry at their parent for seemingly abandoning them, or they may feel like their space is invaded when your loved one is initially released and moves back home. These potential feelings need to be discussed before they happen.

Consider talking with your children about how they feel about their father or mother coming back from prison. Talk to them about how life is about forgiveness. Focus on teaching them that when someone does something wrong, they must face the consequences, forgive themselves, and change for the better.

8. Consider Relationship Counseling

If it is your husband or wife being released from prison, your relationship is about to experience a sudden change, much like the sudden change you felt when he or she was initially incarcerated. There will be excitement and joy with this change, but there are also certain aspects of your relationship that need to be discussed. Relationship counseling will help you and your loved one identify what needs to be resolved and how to work through them in the easiest way possible.

Talk with your husband or wife about finding a local relationship counselor and prepare a few topics or questions you would like to explore with your counselor and loved one.

Needs Of Ex-Prisoners

DISCOVER THE TYPES OF SUPPORT A FORMER PRISONER MIGHT NEED WHEN RETURNING HOME.

Every year, approximately 700,000 men and women are released from U.S. prisons. That's the equivalent of about 2,000 ex-prisoners a day returning to communities across the country.

Going home after being in prison is a very challenging transition for most newly released prisoners, as well as their families and communities. Recidivism studies show that without intervention, two-thirds of those released will return to prison within three years. Sadly, prisoners often go back to prison not because they committed a crime, but because they simply violated parole.

To break this cycle, an effective reentry ministry must consider the needs in all areas of the returning citizen's life: social, intellectual, spiritual, emotional, environmental, and physical. These are the most common needs of a newly released person returning to your community.

IMMEDIATE NEEDS OF EX-PRISONERS

- Safe housing
- Adequate food
- Clothing and personal care items
- Transportation
- A church home
- Emotional and spiritual support
- Proper identification
- Access to a phone
- Medical and dental care; psychiatric care
- Alcohol or substance-abuse treatment and rehabilitation

ONGOING NEEDS OF EX-PRISONERS

- Life-skills training and preparation
- Employment
- Income to cover ongoing expenses
- Further educational and/or vocational training
- Professional services (attorney, accountant, counselor, etc.)
- Mentoring and spiritual guidance/support
- Counseling for family and marital problems
- Strong friendships

PHASES OF REENTRY

Take a look at three vital phases of the ex-prisoner's long journey home.

For many prisoners, the months prior to release are a time of intense fear and insecurity. This time of duress is sometimes referred to as "gate fever." The truth is the problems awaiting former prisoners are often overwhelming. They are not returning to the same world they left behind – things have changed. Their family and friends have gone on with life. Neighborhoods have grown older. Prices have increased on everything.

Technology has become more challenging. Nothing is the same. For years, decisions were made for them by the Department of Corrections. They were told what to eat, what to wear, where to go, and what to do. Now suddenly the former prisoner must make a myriad of decisions about life in the free world–a place that may no longer feel like home, but more like a foreign country.

A PHASED APPROACH

The challenge for reentry ministry volunteers is to be prepared to support returning prisoners during their long journey home. This journey actually begins months before they walk out of the prison gate.

Reentry ministry is best accomplished through a phased approach.

These are three basic phases of successful reentry:

- **PREPARATION:** Beginning 6 to 12 months prior to release, volunteers focus on equipping the prisoner with skills, education, and resources needed to make a successful transition to the outside world. This usually involves coordination between in-prison ministry volunteers and reentry volunteers. The primary goal is for the prisoner to have a detailed reentry plan in place before the expected release date.

- **TRANSITION:** When the ex-prisoner leaves the prison gates, reentry volunteers make sure he or she has safe housing, food, clothing, and many other key supports. During the early days of release, most ex-prisoners need daily encouragement and assistance until their initial crisis-level needs are resolved. Then they need continued weekly contact, spiritual guidance, and emotional support for 6 to 12 months as they find employment, begin to rebuild relationships, and adapt to their new life.

- **STABILIZATION:** Volunteers continue to disciple and assist the ex-prisoner toward establishing consistent personal habits, healthy relationships, spiritual growth, and church commitment. One very important sign of stabilization is when the ex-prisoner becomes involved in serving others in the community instead of expecting to be served. This phase usually takes 12 to 24 months.

Successful reentry ministry involves addressing the needs in all areas of the returning citizen's life: social, intellectual, spiritual, emotional, environmental, and physical. It is possible for a person to be stable in one area of life, but barely surviving in another.

CHEF T'S FINAL THOUGHTS AND INSPIRATION FOR YOU

Your reintegration back into the community will be one of the most challenging things you face. You must understand and embrace this reality. It is important because when your expectations do not line up with reality, then your foundation will be shaken. But, if you are prepared for the inevitable, and that is, the struggle, then your mindset will be prepared. The Art of War says, "If you prepare for 100 battles of 100, then success will be found in all 100." Preparation for the struggle will position you to become empowered during the struggle. You were designed to succeed and you will unveil this success by enduring the uphill climb that all success entails. So, strap on your climbing boots and let's begin this journey with a new mind and a new outlook on life.

You are not alone but are surrounded by the resources that will push and pull you through this journey called life. The only requirement? Faith that leads to action. God will meet you halfway and, for most, this is the greatest stumbling block to the discovery of their success. Most want something for nothing and the universe requires a fair exchange. So, nurture that inner greatness through study, positive peer groups, and a persistent pursuit for developing as many problem-solving skills as possible and watch how your life transforms first from the inside…and, then in the world around you. Remember: we do not get out of life what we want…rather, we get what we are!

AS A PAROLEE, WHAT YOU HAVE TO LOOK FORWARD TO

Day One - Week One

In the days leading up to your release, it is an emotional rollercoaster ride. For those who have served long-term confinement with a strong support system, you will discover that there will be many plans made by those awaiting your return. For those who have a vision, goals, and plans, this monumental day in your life could turn into a frustrating experience. But, it doesn't have to be. Think of yourself as "water" that is able to adjust to your new surroundings. Before you even set one foot on free land, you may have several dinners or get- togethers all planned for you. You may experience family or friends that have been waiting decades for your release and, just like you, they have expectations of how life will be with you being home. When those expectations are not met, disappointment sets in. So, be like water and change the habit of trying to control outcomes and instead, focus on process (who you are becoming).

Your excitement and anxiety may allow for a numbness to all the emotions you are experiencing. However, for most, that numbness soon wears off to the realization of a bundle of emotions, from emptiness, due to the loss of a sense of purpose or friendships. That first week will begin with the highest moment possible and end in the realization that the "fight" has just begun.

1 month - 3 months

If you have a vision, or goals, or plans, couple it with action upon your release. You should have a driver's license (or have achieved measurable actions towards it), registered for a vocational trade/skill and/or completed your Free Application for Federal Student Aid (FAFSA) with an intentional plan aimed at a livable wage career, and connect with job opportunities that will help push you towards your career (Education, 2018).

Your emotional state will begin a process of decompression from the conditioning of the super aggressive environment you've been freed from. This first month will be challenging, yet understanding this, will empower you to prepare and better understand what to expect and how best to respond. You have been conditioned to respond to stress and conflict with aggression and violence. That response helped push you through the obstacles you faced in prison. You are coming from an environment where winning every verbal or physical fight was essential for survival.

Out here, those who resolve conflict that allows for all "winners", that is a "win-win-win", masters the skill and artistry of influence. And he who leads through permission and the benefit of all those around him, increases his problem-solving skills and therefore, his paycheck. Don't forget, "keeping it real" can keep you broke. During this beginning phase, exercise the mantra "there is no fight"...and "no one is my friend or enemy, but everyone is my teacher".

3 months - 6 months

During this phase of your reintegration, you will begin to discover what you "don't like", whether it be food, relationships, jobs, and certain environments. This is good. Remember that whatever pushes you closer to your vision and goals is what you should spend your most valuable resource (time) on. If you sow the right seed now, then your harvest will be according to your plans. Be conscious in how and with whom you are spending your days. It is normal during this phase to stagnate (slow down or even stop) in your progress and pursuit for all that you envisioned and planned. The reason is because now you are in space where every vision must be tested and every goal challenged. Just remember: You can only see the stars in the darkness. So, the darker (unsure) the path gets, the more you must maintain consistent action towards your vision and goals. Feelings mean nothing and principles everything during the hardest of your times.

6 months - 1 year

During this time, if you are following your vision, goals, and plans, then life is not getting easier, but you are getting stronger socially (in how you interact with the world around you), emotionally (your emotional intelligence is stretching to respond to triggers and stress pro-socially), and mentally (you are expanding your knowledge of skills that can expand your income). Every level will have new "devils" and your success will always depend not on what happens "to you" but how you respond to it! That is your mantra during this phase: "It is not what happens to me, but how I respond to it that determines my success!"

You must continue to grow and expand your communication skills that allow you to create, maintain, and restore your relationships, which is called "interpersonal skills". Your ability to create strong relationships through effective interpersonal skills will determine how high you climb personally and professionally. Your ability to respond effectively to daily conflict, which is inevitable, will determine your income. Remember that a job is solving a problem at an agreed upon price-point. So, if you want to increase that price-point then you must continue to increase your problem-solving skills.

The greatest problem solvers are those who are able to influence conflict in a way that empowers the mission, aims, and goals. Expand your problem-solving skills and watch your income expand. Internships and low paying jobs may sound uninviting yet remember that it is not what you get but who you become in the process. So, an internship will help shape you into the problem solver that attracts a higher income because it is process (learning the position) over product (the low paying internship/job).

THE TURN
AROUND PLACE
Chef Tee

Chapter 6 –
Societal Problems

Assessed by Julius E. Hoggard, B.A., M.B.A., QMHP

Problem: Glorification of Substance Abuse Amongst Celebrities

Effect:

Celebrities and substance abuse plays a large role in shaping the expectations, approach, and behavior regarding substance abuse. Excessive use and abuse of a substance is linked to periods of rapid social change. Behind Celebrities and substance abuse's influence, exists an impact from a person's cultural roots— the country in which they originated from has an influence on the social norms they have learned. For example, a person greatly influenced by the current Celebrities and substance abuse climate may have pre-existing values taken from their country of origin, like the French, who drink wine with dinner nightly and enjoy a bottle of wine when socializing with friends.

An audience interprets anything seen in Celebrities and substance abuse, whether it be an example or thought-provoking, Celebrities and substance abuse speaks to us, and we listen. Celebrities and substance abuse is inescapable, it is everywhere— in the press, on the radio, in films and television, in print, and on the internet. It is impossible to be plugged into any form of social media without seeing what Celebrities and substance abuse is.

Drug culture is a subculture of Celebrities and substance abuse, it represents the principles, patterns, physicality, hierarchy, and behavior within a group of individuals with substance use disorders. We see drug culture in various movies, television shows, music, etc. Drug culture has a hierarchy, dependent on your role in the community of drug users; you can be a drug synthesizer, supplier, dealer, and user. Drug culture is made up of socialization, values, rules, gender roles and relationships, symbols and images, dress, language and communication, and attitudes.

In addition to drug cultures, there are also drinking cultures. Think college sororities and fraternities, where it is a part of their culture to drink in massive quantities, supports binge drinking, reinforces denial, develops rituals and customary behaviors around drinking (Center for Substance Abuse Treatment). Many people turn to subcultures like drug and drinking cultures as a source of social support and cultural activities that make these people feel like they belong somewhere, or "fit in."

The danger of subcultures like these is the toleration and promotion of harmful activities like using drugs and alcohol to socialize. Socializing no longer becomes the objective, but using drugs and alcohol together becomes the objective—with socialization being an after effect. A lot of anti-social behavior is supported, which includes opposition to authority, rule-breaking, defiance, and destructive acts, among other behaviors. Many further specified subcultures can stem from the broader drug or alcohol culture. "The need for social acceptance is a major reason many young people begin to use drugs, as social acceptance can be found with less effort within the drug culture" (Center for Substance Abuse Treatment).

Solution:

There are multiple solutions that can be helpful in the upliftment in society, particularly in the African American community when it comes to the glorification of substance abuse by entertainers and influencers within the celebrity world, whether they are music artists, sports athletes, movie actors, politicians, community activists, etc. We must, as an entire community, hold liable of the effects the entire music and entertainment industry has on its followers such as the African American community. We must use extended education on the youth, in particularly on the harmful effects of using illicit drugs, and alcohol. We must also hold accountability to the many influencers and celebrities that have a negative effect on the use of drugs and alcohol and how its influence our community.

Additionally, one can hold the parent, or guardian accountable to such standards as well. Parents/Guardians play a significant role in the influence of drugs and alcohol. Parents can literally impact the actions of the youth if one pays attention to the warning signs. Parents must monitor the children's social media periodically, to ensure that their children are not getting merely influenced by drug and alcohol abuse from what and who they follow on social media.

When it comes to the trend of celebrities, particularly in the African American culture of hip-hop music, oftentimes youth imitate what they see on social media, internet, TV, etc. In the perspective of honesty, children are innocent, until they are influenced. Children or youth attached themselves to what they see daily. If one sees praises of glorification of drugs and alcohol, that can very well be what that youth attach to currently or soon.

The effects of glorifying alcohol and drug culture has ripped in particularly the African American community apart substantially. Substance abuse has broken family homes, children separate from parents; Mothers and Fathers in treatment facilities and ordered to complete programs to qualify and be parents again. Generation after generation the cycle continues from the impact of glorification of drugs and alcohol, with the influence of the entire entertainment industry playing an important role.

Solutions are there and we as an entire community must hold each other accountable, whether they are loved ones, family members, co-workers, friends, etc., we must get in a space where love is centered around telling the truth and holding each other accountable about one's actions. Honesty is key, and very important in combating the harmful effects on the influence of substance abuse amongst minorities and celebrity influencers.

As Chef T. Wallace has often stated to the youth and even adults; "How can a celebrity come from working as an officer in the criminal justice system, to being an important celebrity figure, and promote the violence, drugs, and alcohol that he currently promotes." Too often that narrative of a statement may be true. Often celebrities/ influencers promote lifestyles that they may not significantly indulge into daily. So, we must remember that the influencers (whether they are music artists, athletes, actors, etc.) are human too. They also go through trials and tribulations that we know anything about when it comes to the use of illicit drugs and substance abuse. We must support and assist each other for the statistics to show as a community, we have prevented a large percentage of addicts, and substance abuse users in the African American community. With the right resources, tools, and leaders, we can do it; however, we must be willing to accomplish the task!

<u>A Few Celebrities That Have Passed Away from Substance Abuse</u>

1. Jimi Hendrix- died from a sleeping pill overdose-Age 27

2. Whitney Houston-died from cocaine-Age 48

3. Michael Jackson-died from Benzodiazepines-Age 50

4. Prince-died from Fentanyl-Age 57

5. Heath Ledger-died from prescription drugs-Age 28

It is noted that a large percentage of celebrities that have passed away from the use of substance abuse have not had charitable foundations, nonprofit organizations, etc., in their honor/name when it comes specifically dealing with substance abuse within the community. We must as a collective community address the crisis concerning substance abuse within the culture that we embrace. Substance abuse is glorified in almost every aspect of our current culture, whether it's in the music & entertainment industry, actor/actress, athlete, social media star, etc., substance abuse has become an important concern currently, and throughout future generations to come. Combating substance abuse within the community will take time that will not happen overnight with positive results. It will have to take initiative to secure victory in this long fight that communities in society have been facing for decades. We must understand the root cause of the substance and drug culture within our community first. We must tackle that first to understand the next step to achieve success in combating drug and substance abuse that so effectively has a firm grip within our society.

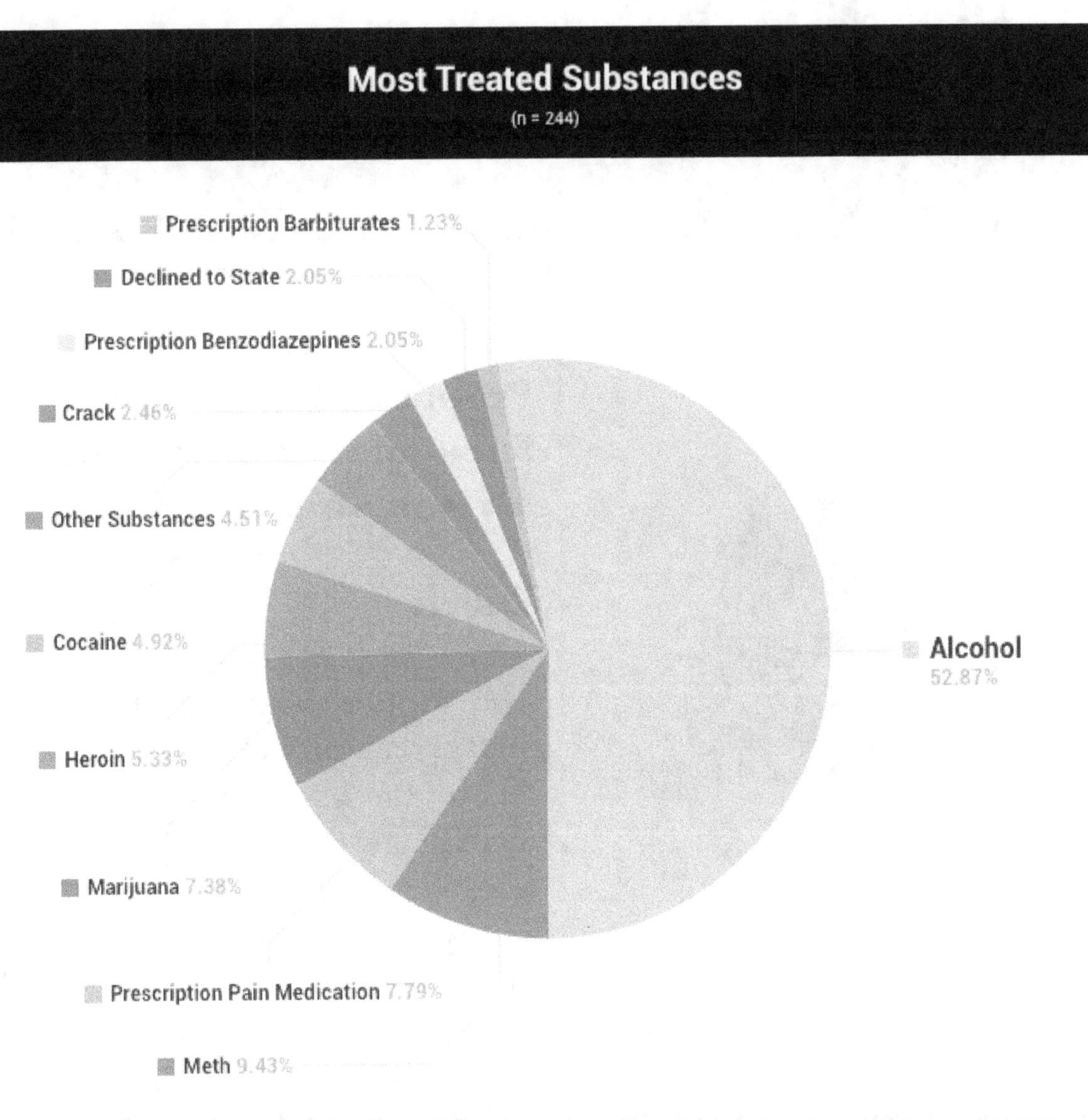

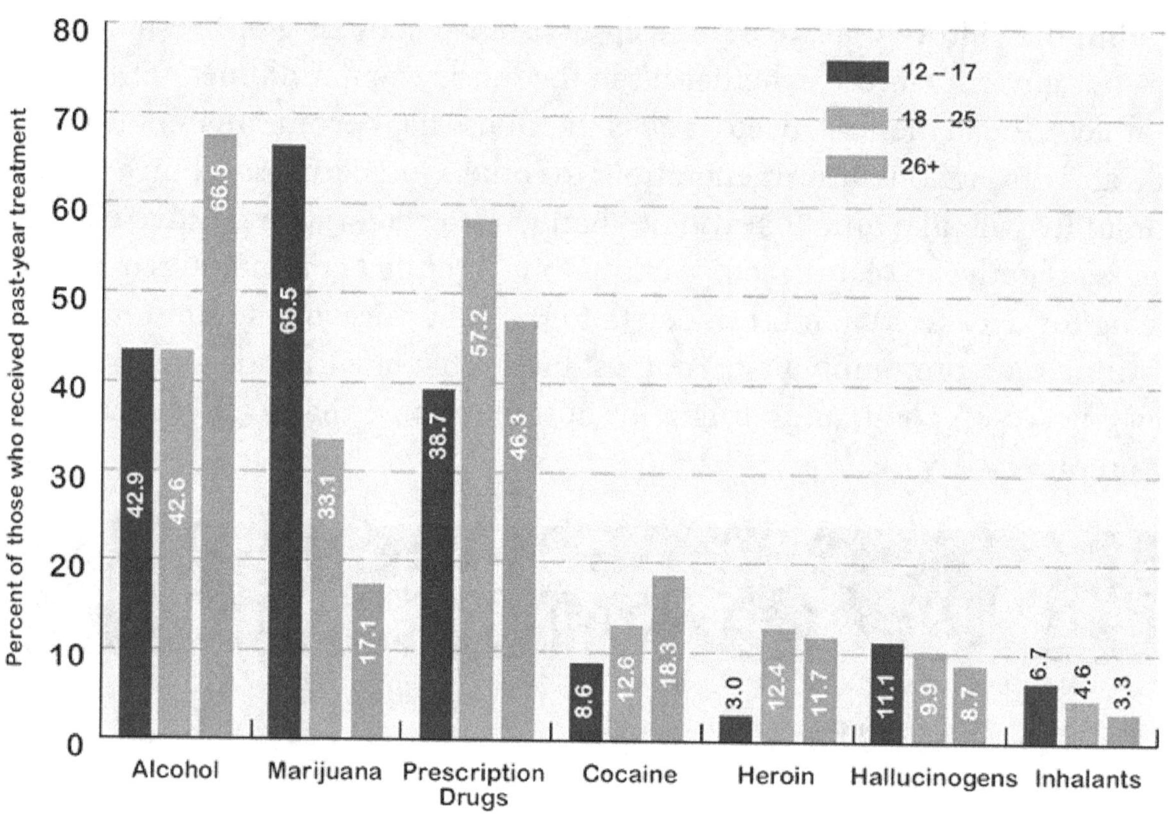

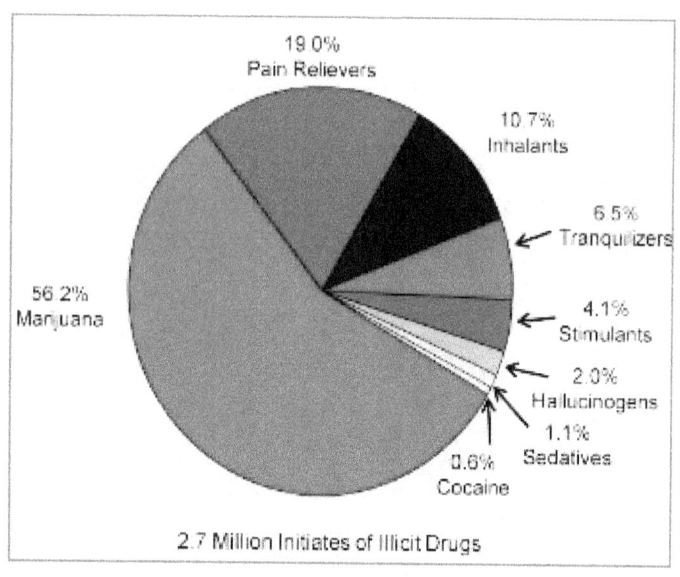

Problem: The Effects of Substance Abuse within the African American Community

Effect:

The disproportionate and devastating impact that alcohol and other drug use has had on the Black community is becoming increasingly clear as is the need for rigorous research on the causes of this inequity and ways to prevent it. Society must first understand the culture and diversity of the African American community and identify ways to effectively involve families and communities in efforts to prevent substance abuse. Increased efforts must be made to understand and reinforce protective factors, such as religious and church activity, education, employment, family support, communal orientations, and ethnic pride. Additionally, the field of drug abuse prevention would be greatly enhanced by the increased involvement of African American researchers and professionals who have a vested interest in the needs of the population and have a greater advantage in overcoming community barriers. The specific needs of the Black community must be understood and addressed if we are to overcome the disproportionate burden alcohol and other drug use imposes on this community.

Risk of drug use increases greatly during times of transition. For an adult, a divorce or loss of a job may increase the risk of drug use. For a teenager, risky times include moving, family divorce, or changing schools. When children advance from elementary through middle school, they face new and challenging social, family, and academic situations. Often during this period, children are exposed to substances such as cigarettes and alcohol for the first time. When they enter high school, teens may encounter greater availability of drugs, drug use by older teens, and social activities where drugs are used. When individuals leave high school and live more independently, either in college or as an employed adult, they may find themselves exposed to drug use while separated from the protective structure provided by family and school.

The opioid crisis has had devastating effects on communities all over the country—with challenges for communities of color. According to the U.S. Centers for Disease Control and Prevention, the largest percentage increase of drug overdose and deaths in recent years has been among African Americans, who often face more barriers to treatment than the general population when factoring in stigma, bias, and socioeconomic status.

In the United States, about 51% of older adolescents and adults have used illegal drugs or illegally diverted prescription drugs over their lifetimes, and about 15% have used them over the prior 12 months. In a recent national study among adults, prevalence rates for any substance disorder were 14.6% for lifetime, and 3.8% for the prior 12 months. Studies of racial and ethnic differences have found that Whites have higher prevalence rates of substance abuse disorders than do other racial and ethnic groups, but racial and ethnic minorities have been shown to have substance abuse disorders that persist for longer periods of time. Findings from the National Survey on Drug Use and Health also showed higher drug abuse rates for Whites than for racial or ethnic minorities, except for abuse of crack cocaine and heroin. Despite the lifetime and current prevalence rates of illegal drug use being lower for Blacks, Blacks are overrepresented in the health and criminal justice systems.

Solution:

For people who have already begun using drugs or have already increased their use to the point of abuse, the best solution is to begin treatment. There are certain risk factors that increase the chances a person will begin abusing drugs. These risk factors include having a family history of drug abuse or alcohol abuse, being exposed to people who commonly use drugs, living in poverty, underachieving in school, having a mental health disorder such as ADHD, depression, and being able to easily access drugs.

The biggest reason teens start using illicit drugs is because their friends utilize peer pressure. No one likes to be left out, and teens (and yes, some adults, too) find themselves doing things they normally wouldn't do, just to fit in. In these cases, you need to either find a better group of friends that won't pressure you into doing harmful things, or you need to find a good way to say no. Teens should prepare a good excuse or plan of time, to keep from giving into tempting situations. People today are overworked and overwhelmed, and often feel like a good break or a reward is deserved. But in the end, drugs only make life more stressful — and many of us all too often fail to recognize this in the moment. To prevent using drugs as a reward, find other ways to handle stress and unwind. Take up exercising, read a good book, volunteer with the needy, create something. Anything positive and relaxing helps take the mind off using drugs to relieve stress. Mental illness and substance abuse often go together. Those with a mental health illness may turn to drugs to ease the pain. Those suffering from some form of mental health illness, such as anxiety, depression or post-traumatic stress disorder should seek support and professional help before it leads to substance use.

If you're aware of the biological, environmental, and physical risk factors you possess, you're more likely to overcome them. A history of substance abuse in the family, living in a social setting that glorifies drug abuse and/or family life that models drug abuse can be risk factors.

People take up drugs when something in their life is not working, or when they're unhappy about their lives or where their lives are going. Look at life's big picture and have priorities in order.

There are many options and solutions that can impact substance abuse with the African American community. Resources such as treatment centers, therapist, life coaches, recreational centers, community leaders, etc., all can play an impactful role in the development of next generation of African Americans to not rely solely on substance abuse because of the circumstances one may be facing, along with other mental health issues that have direct connections with substance abuse users. Community programs such as AA/NA meetings are very impactful; however, a real addict or substance abuse user needs to have access to many more resources so that they can have a fighting chance with tackling substance abuse 24/7 around the clock.

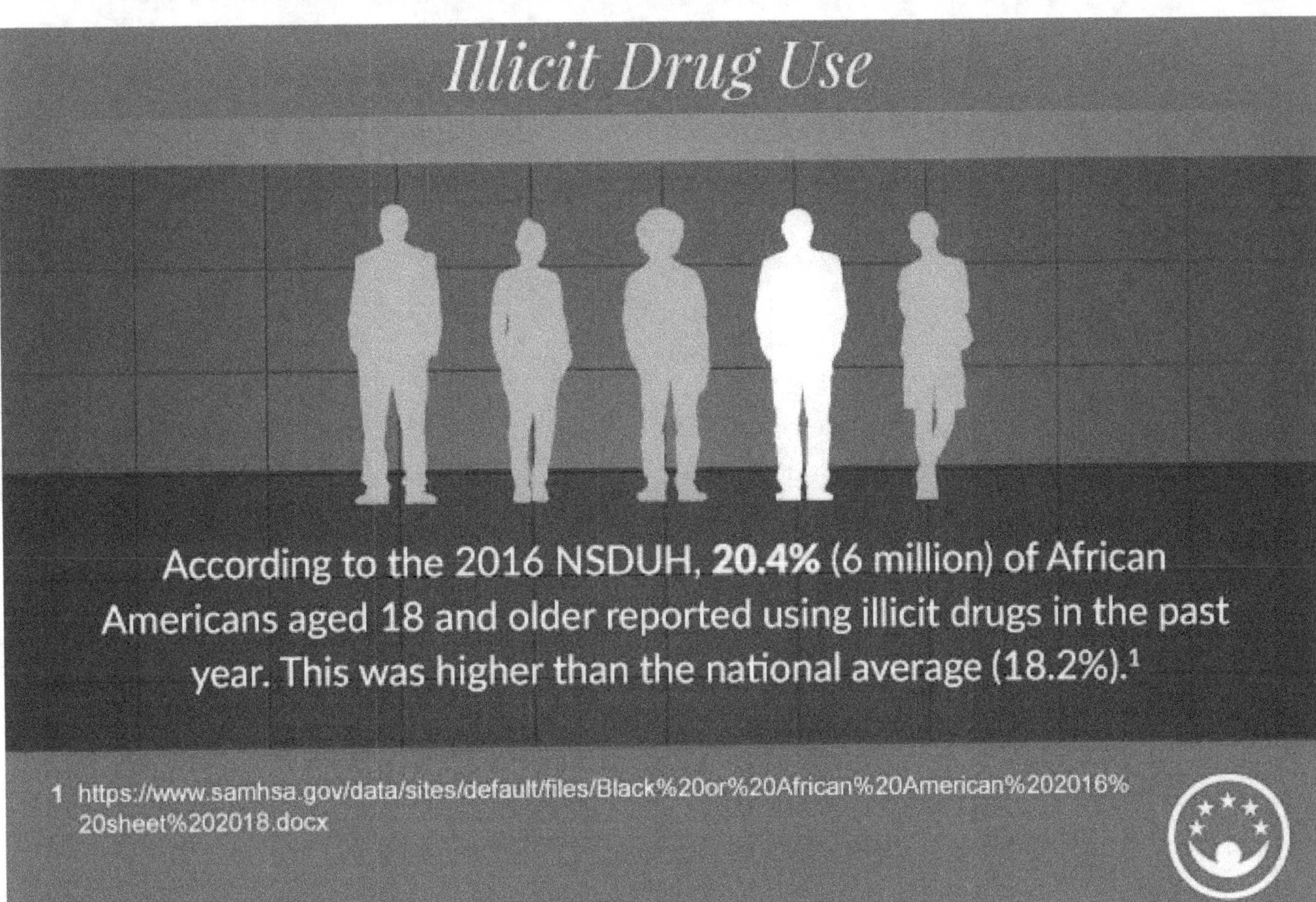

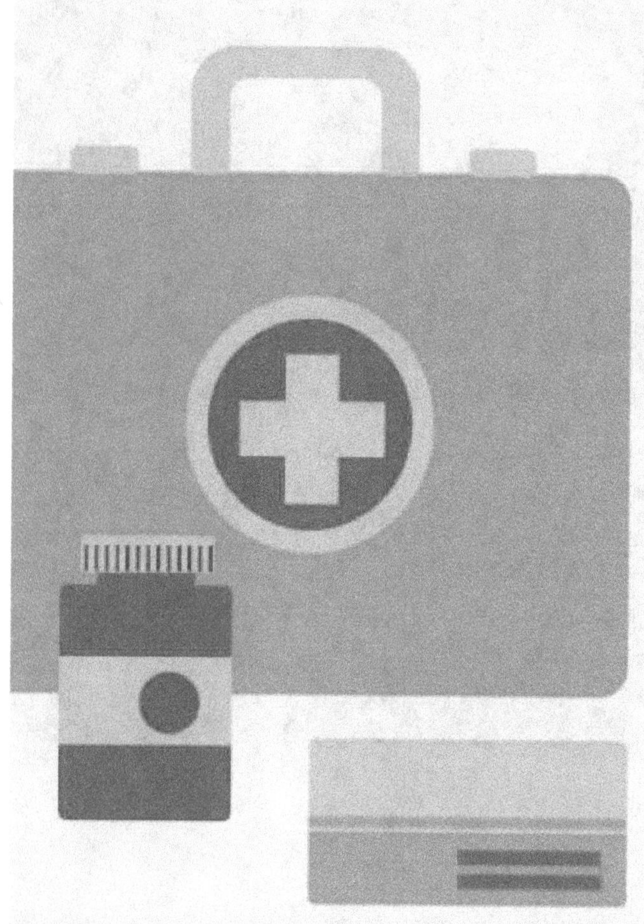

RECEIVING TREATMENT

- Among those Americans who needed treatment for illicit drug use, **21.3%** of blacks received treatment at a specialty facility, compared to **17.3%** of the rest of the population.

- **9.1%** of African Americans need specialty treatment for substance abuse, compared to **9.3%** of the rest of the population.

- **15.2%** of those that need treatment go on to receive treatment, compared to **9.6%** of the rest of the population.[1]

1 https://www.samhsa.gov/data/sites/default/files/NSDUH124/NSDUH124/sr124-african-american-treatment.htm

The Effects of Stereotypes

17 Million

Whites reported having used an illicit drug within the last month

4 Million

Blacks reported having used an illicit drug within the last month

Although African Americans make up only **12.5%** of illicit drug users, **33%** of drug incarcerations are black. This leads to major roadblocks in treatments for substance abuse among the population, as there is a fear in self-reporting.[1]

1 https://www.naacp.org/criminal-justice-fact-sheet/

Problem: Undiagnosed Developmental and Learning Disabilities and Lack of Securing Proper Support

Effect:

Treating children with learning disorders is a significant challenge. A complete and accurate history is therefore crucial. The early years are very important. Issues of poverty and neglect are just as important currently (Evans, 2004; Garber & Begab, 1988; McCain & Mustard, 1999) as they were in previous decades (White, 1975). Early neglect impairs brain growth and development (Haydar, 2005) and produces mild mental retardation (MMR), but seldom is the effect of poverty and neglect integrated with our understanding of the etiology of prominent specific learning disorders such as learning disabilities (LDs), attention deficit hyperactivity disorder (ADHD).

For some children, parents cannot fill these roles as buffer and co-regulator effectively. When children have caregivers who cannot buffer them from stress or who cannot serve as co-regulators, they are vulnerable to the vicissitudes of a challenging environment. Although children can cope effectively with mild or moderate stress when supported by a caregiver, conditions that exceed their capacities to cope adaptively often result in problematic short- or long-term consequences.

These consequences could lead to other disorders such as mental health from the Individual. The feeling of not being wanted or accepted by family members or/ and community can be very detrimental for the Individual mental health and overall health. Social issues such as poverty, and lack of resources can be key issues in the adversity of supporting Individuals with learning/developmental disabilities. Children who have experienced abuse and neglect are therefore at increased risk for several problematic developmental, health, and mental health outcomes, including learning problems (e.g., problems with inattention and deficits in executive functions), problems relating to peers (e.g., peer rejection), internalizing symptoms (e.g., depression, anxiety), externalizing symptoms (e.g., oppositional defiant disorder, conduct disorder, aggression), and posttraumatic stress disorder (PTSD). As adults, these children continue to show increased risk for psychiatric disorders, substance use, serious medical illnesses, and lower economic productivity.

Solution:

Today there are concerns on proper support for undiagnosed developmental and learning disabilities amongst our community. We must tackle this lack of support and make it better for the next generation of Individuals that have some form of disability whether it is related to developmental or learning. There are great services for these Individuals in place currently. However, there are gaps that need to be filled concerning the lack of support a large percentage of Individuals experience whether residing inside a home, community center, group home, day support, etc. The main point is to acknowledge that we, whether we are Providers, Professionals, Therapists, Teachers, etc., are very essential to the correct support, that are needed to provide the best possible services to the Individuals we serve. Learning disabilities are NOT mental retardation, nor are they the result of a poor academic background, emotional disturbance, lack of motivation, or visual or auditory acuity problems (Association of Higher Education and Disability). A person with a learning disability may have average or above average intelligence.

Some suggestions say that better quality training may be proper to ensure an increasing number of customer satisfaction to the Individuals we serve. Adequate training such as Human Rights, HIPPA Training, First Aid/CPR, Crisis Management, etc., could be targeted trainings to Professionals and others, that seek to want to make a positive difference within the Individuals we serve. One must understand, that the very way a person has a developmental or learning disability, could have been the way one of our dear family members could be displayed. When dealing with Individuals with developmental/learning disabilities, one must treat the Individual as one would want a very special loved one to be treated. We must be educated, but compassionate concerning the issues involving Individuals with undiagnosed developmental and learning disabilities.

FIGURE 1.

"Thinking back, what could have been improved about your transition from high school to college?"

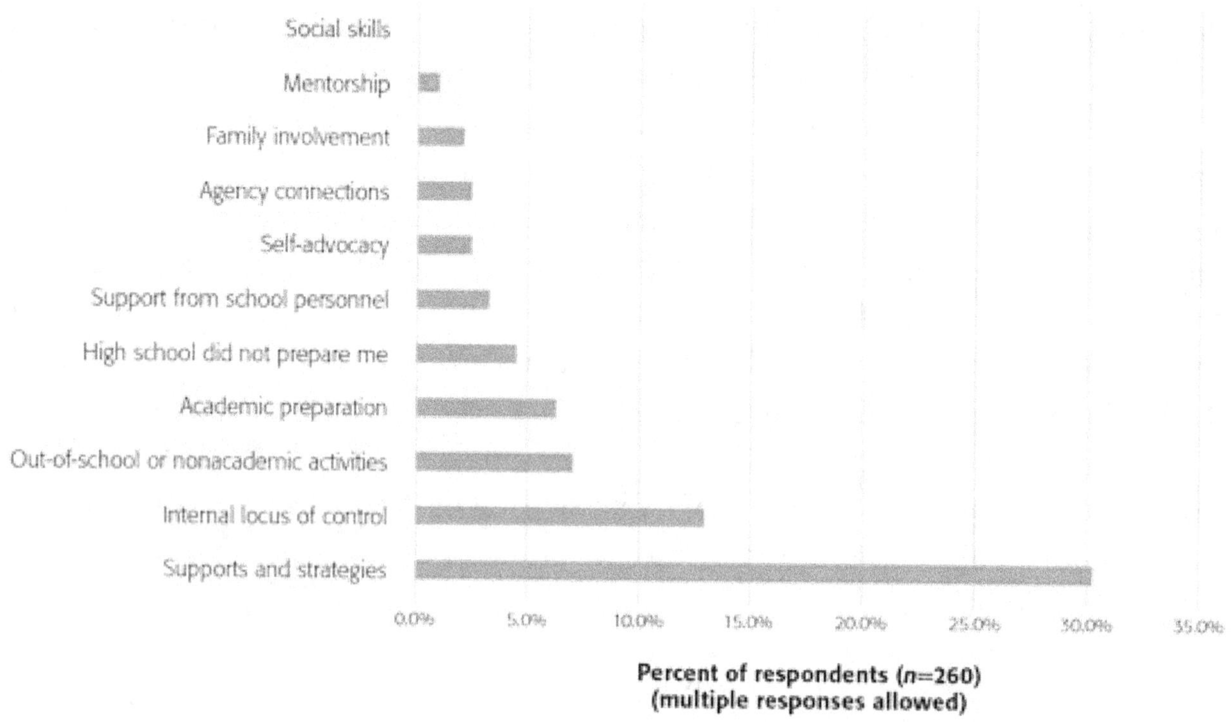

Social skills
Mentorship
Family involvement
Agency connections
Self-advocacy
Support from school personnel
High school did not prepare me
Academic preparation
Out-of-school or nonacademic activities
Internal locus of control
Supports and strategies
0.0%
5.0%
10.0%
15.0%
20.0%
25.0%
30.0%
35.0%
Percent of respondents (n=260)
(multiple responses allowed)

Diagnosis
2.5
0.6
11.1
11.8
73.9
SLD
GLD
Language Difficulties
Mixed-type Learning Disorders
Other types of comorbidity

(a)

Types of SLD
14.7
26.6
16.2
0
42.5
Reading
Written expression
Mathematics
Mixed
Other

(b)

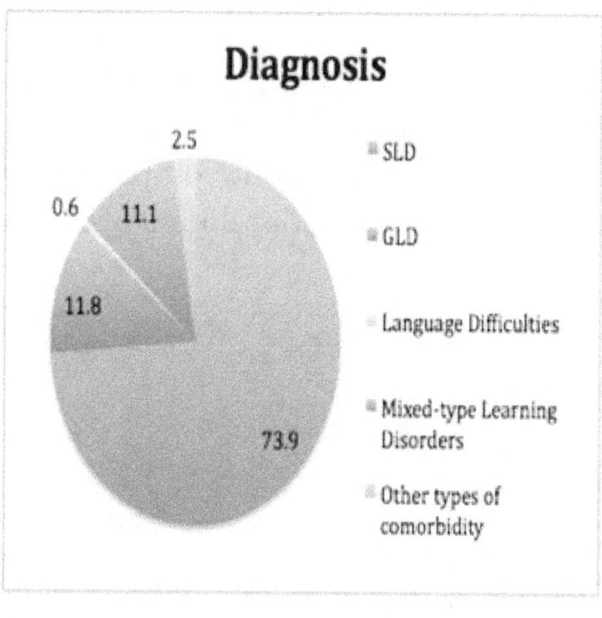

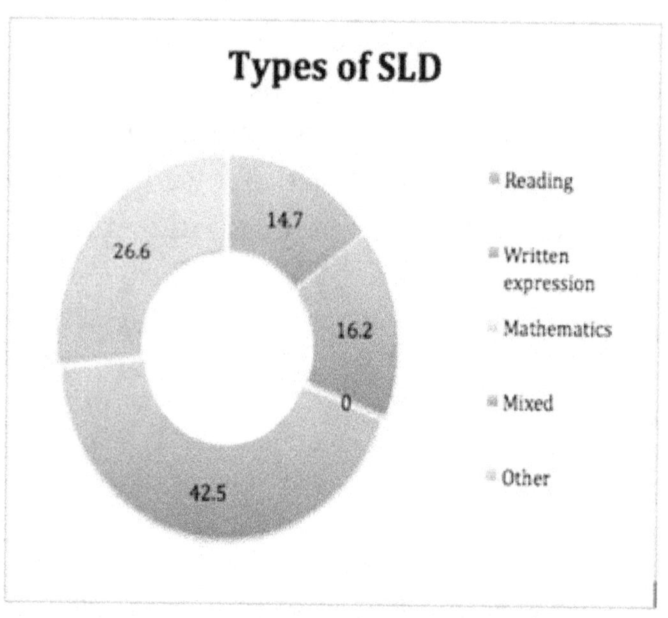

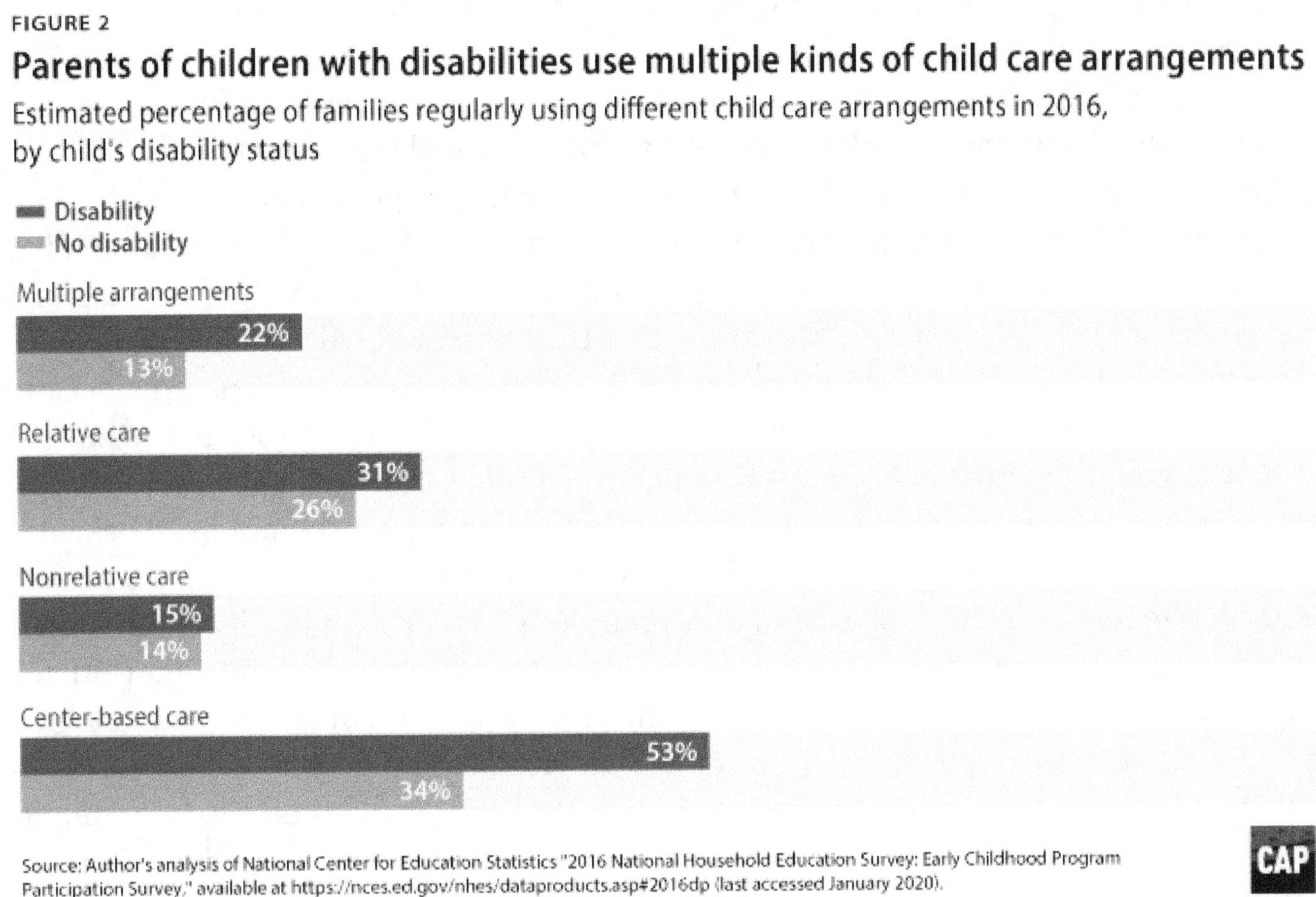

Source: Author's analysis of National Center for Education Statistics "2016 National Household Education Survey: Early Childhood Program Participation Survey," available at https://nces.ed.gov/nhes/dataproducts.asp#2016dp (last accessed January 2020).

Problem: Absentee Parents

Effect:

One of the issues that we find in our society today, is the absence of the biological father or the lack of a father figure in the home and/or the lives of children. For clarification, I would like to say that parents do not have to be in a marriage or in a relationship to support their children, but parents must have a positive relationship. Parents can successfully co-parent without living in the same home; however, a healthy functional two parent household is the most idealistic.

According to the Pew Center, the statistics show that the number of children not in two parent household is significantly higher than the 1970's. What happens to our youth when they lack the support and presence of both parents? Sometimes the result of this is children feel a lack of support because one or both parents are absent. The result is sometimes feeling lack of love and belonging.

Concerning our youth lacking the support of one or both parents can significantly be a factor due to the decline of traditional two-parent households. The effect this phenomenon has is often a negative one when it comes to the statistics. Economic resources play an important role in parent's ability to provide the material resources for children to thrive into society. When a child feels lack of support because one or both parents are absent can take a serious unfortunate turn. Unfortunately, some children involve themselves with a dangerous group of individuals whether they are crews, gangs, etc. Another effect is the lack of balance within the household when there are absentee parents. Balance is very important when raising a child between two parents because of what both parents naturally can do pertaining to their children. Society has become so accustomed to non-traditional family values, that today it seems having a traditional two-parent household is not important as it was in the recent past. Children are learner's whatever environment they are in. A large percentage of absentee parent homes can be related to the uptick of problems in the community, especially minority communities, where poverty and gangs have a deep role. Poverty in the household unfortunately can lead to children experiencing trauma and mental health issues early on. Being a product of your environment can impact children's logical thinking, especially when one is poor. Crime and poverty have direct ties to each other in the minority community. Street gangs are tied into crime and poverty, which a large percentage of children join because of the lack of moral support or love within their own homes. This phenomenon has led to generation after generation of minority communities feeling the impact of crime and violence in their community and homes. Children tend to be attracted to this phenomenon because of what they see on TV and social media as of late. Social media has children believing that being a part of a life where crime, and violence is the new normal for them because of the lack of opportunities that exist within their own communities.

Solution:

There are solutions that can be bought to the attention of parents or upcoming parents to heed to. Some solutions can work well than others depending on a person's background, mental health status, and educational background just to name a few. A person's background (family history, individual history, etc.) can have a direct impact when children are involved. A person's mental health status plays a factor in how a child(ren) are raised and provided for. Educational background plays a significant role as having a higher education or becoming a tradesman can have both parents on the path to not be in poverty as more completed education such as college, graduate school, etc. can increase a person's annual income in a lifetime. This is very important when it comes to raising children because as a parent, one needs good finances and resources to adequately provide for a child.

Mental health has a major role in raising a child. Studies have shown that mental health is associated with absentee parents. Having mental health doesn't have to be a negative issue. The issue is not having enough support dealing with one's mental health. Children who cannot lean on a parent or parents during difficult times tend to have major mental health problems. Children can face mental health issues because of the lack of support in the household. Parents must be proactive in tackling the issue of mental health concerning their children. Parents must have resources available, such as having access to Community Counselors, Qualified Mental Health Professionals, Therapists, Life Coaches, etc., to decrease the stigma of mental health among absentee parents for their children. Don't be afraid, reach out to agencies and organizations that have resources to combat mental health within the home, schools, and community.

How to nurture a child's mental health

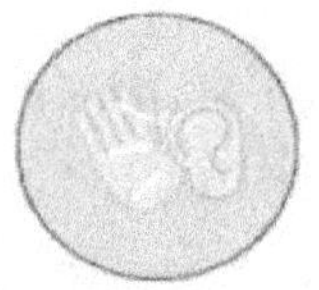

Actively listen before offering your advice

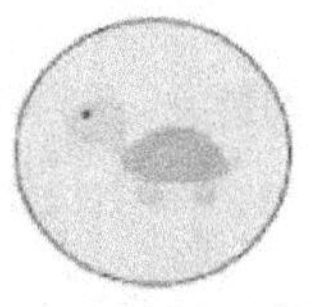

Be patient

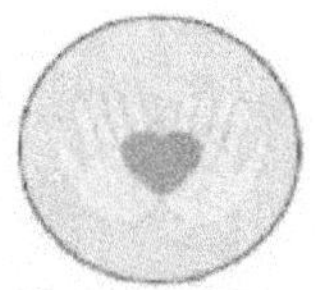

Share your feelings and validate theirs

Tell the truth

Model healthy behavior

Surround them with healthy adults

Teach them how to be safe

Use open ended questions

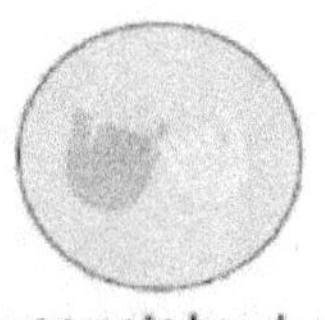

Be consistent and follow through with what you promise

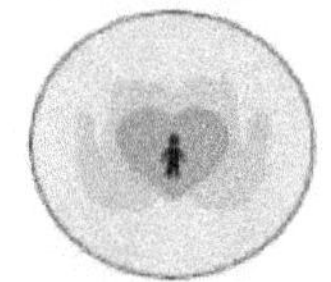

Believe them and in them

Practice relaxation exercises together

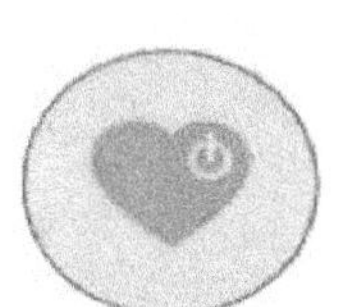

Have scheduled family time

Limit electronic time for everyone

Reach out and hug them

Model forgiveness

Respond calmly when their emotions are elevated

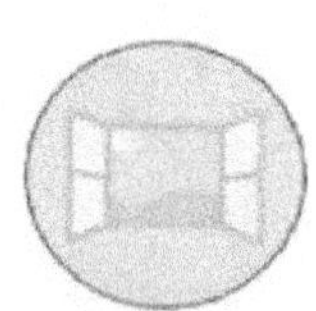

View their behavior as a window to their needs and feelings

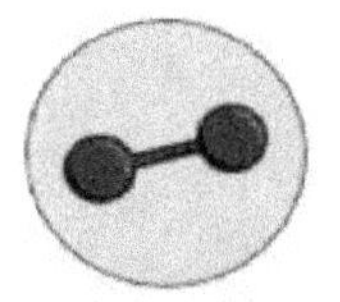

Make play and exercise a requirement

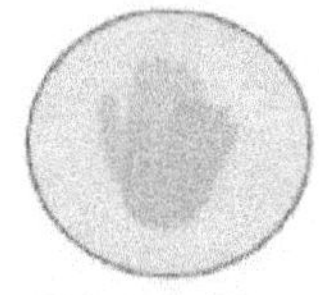

Recognize positive choices

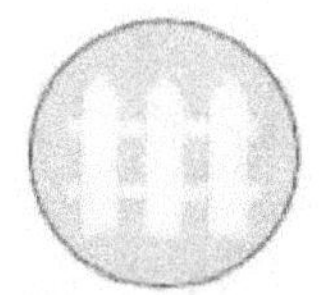

Set and respect boundaries

Be present

Problem: Violence

Effect:

Violence in low-income neighbors where mostly people of color most specifically Blacks and Hispanics reside is one of the biggest threats to their existence. It is not uncommon to ride through these neighborhoods and see several makeshift memorials dedicated to these individuals. These individuals are often young men in their late teens, twenties, and early thirties. For many young men and women who live in these neighborhoods, funerals have become the norm in their families, social circles, and communities at large. It is becoming more commonplace for families to have suffered the loss of several of their youth to violence. The question that we must ask ourselves is why is this happening? Why are our young people so seemingly casually killing each other without pause? There are numerous causes of these acts of violence ranging from gang violence, domestic violence, etc.; however, what is certain is the devastating effect that violence has on the urban community.

The effect of violence is brutal and there is no end to the many effects of violence. One effect that violence can have on the community is that in areas where violence is commonplace many residents most specifically the youth live in constant fear. They have often seen individuals or been in the vicinity of individuals who are brutally killed. They in their innocence have seen people lain on the ground with police tap around the crime scene and white sheets spread over the victim who they often know personally. This creates trauma and post-traumatic stress disorder because the fear is that they or their family and friends could be next. They often jump at the sound of anything perceived to be gunfire and they either make the decision to flee from anything that could result in violence, or they decide to accept it as a way of like and cleave to it. Individuals living in these communities are seldom prepared for these untimely deaths and thus endure financial hardships and stress to bury their family members so those who are already experiencing financial hardship often must take on another financial responsibility of the burial (funeral) expenses of their family members. Another effect is the desensitization of our youth in reference to violence and death, because many of them have lost family members and friends, they often become desensitize to it and don't properly deal with loss of grief, they simply accept it as a way of life. This often results in a lack of hope for the future and many youths in these neighborhoods do not aspire to goals or create plans for themselves because they simply cannot see themselves living beyond their teenage years and/or their circumstance and thus with their lack of hope comes complacency and acceptance of violence as a matter of fact and a way of life.

Solution:

There are several solutions that can be proposed to address this problem and to eradicate the trauma and devastation that comes with it. One stand only solution will not fix the problem, but there must be a collective effort of community members/families, law enforcement, city wide officials/leaders versus just the city officials/leaders representing that ward/area, and various community organizations. Most important is that the community members even those members who are involved in a mindset, belief system, and a lifestyle in which the perpetuation of violence is a way of life must buy into change and evolve from being the problem to being part of the solution.

- Youth Employee Programs
- More vocational/trade programs
- Community Center
- Community Sports Leagues that require little to no monetary contribution from families
- Recommitment to the practice of the village raising the children
- Mentors
- Rehabilitation programs or youth who have been active in gangs

TRACKING AMERICAN POVERTY & POLICY

Number of poor children receiving cash aid: one in five.

Children under age 18 in poverty: 16.4 million, or 22 percent of all children, including 39 percent of African-American children, 35 percent of Latino children, and 12 percent of white children.

39%
35%
12%
African-American children
Latino children
White children

Over the last 50 years, the steepest increase in poverty rates was among children under 5, and those in early adulthood aged 18-24.

Under 5 years old
18-24 year-olds

Single mothers with incomes under $25,000: 50 percent.

Families receiving cash assistance: 27 for every 100 families living in poverty

Economic growth didn't trickle down: Since 1980, GDP has doubled while poverty rates have remained essentially flat.

Dēmos

LEARN MORE AT: WWW.TRACKINGPOVERTYANDPOLICY.ORG | WWW.DEMOS.ORG

Rate of violent victimization, by poverty level and location of residence, 2008–2012

Rate per 1,000 persons age 12 or older

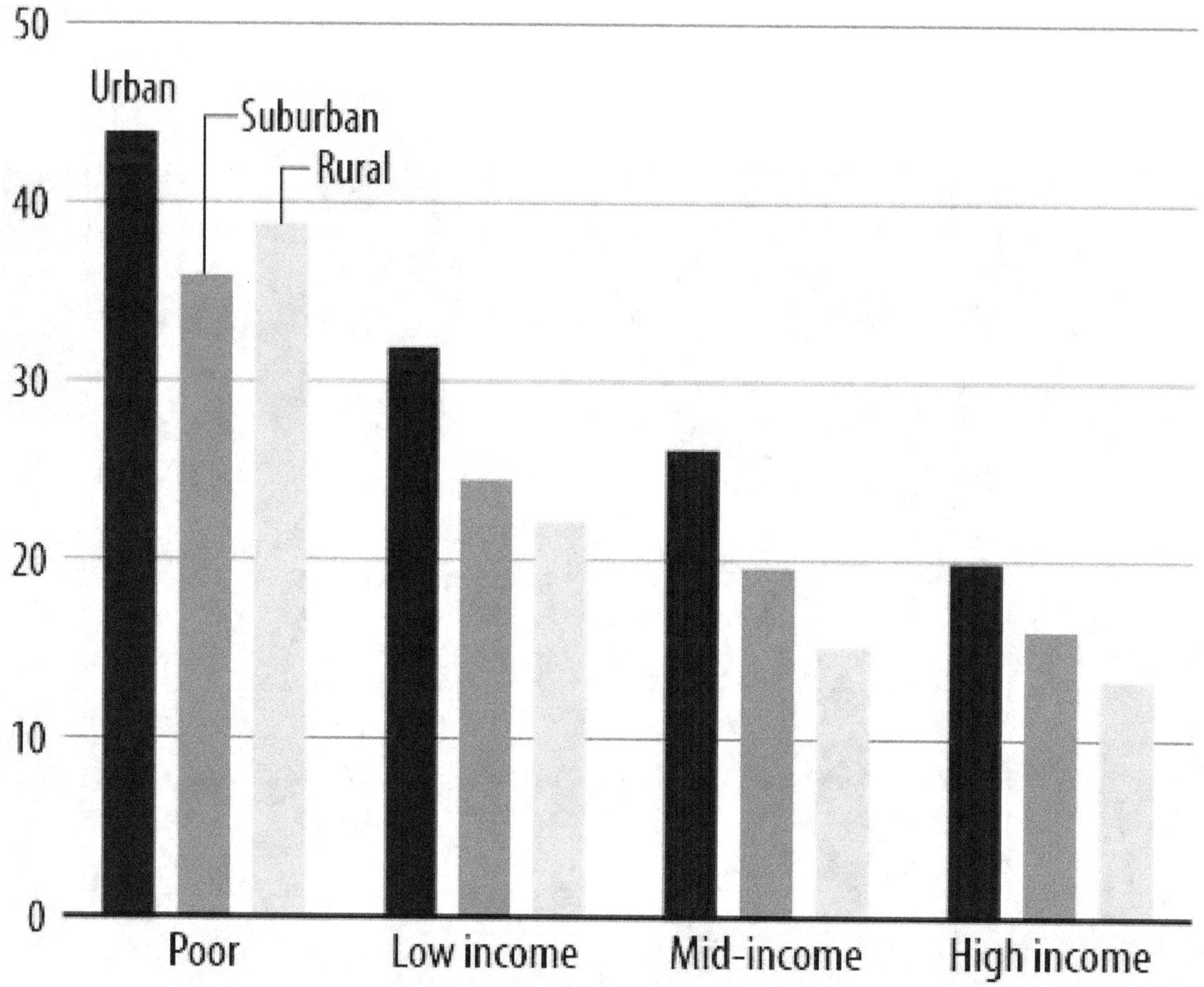

Note: Poor refers to households at 0% to 100% of the Federal Poverty Level (FPL). Low income refers to households at 101% to 200% of the FPL. Mid-income refers to households at 201% to 400% of the FPL. High income refers to households at 401% or higher than the FPL. See appendix table 7 for estimates and standard errors.

Source: Bureau of Justice Statistics, National Crime Victimization Survey, 2008–2012.

Works Cited

Adamson, C. R. (2014, August 2). Punishment After Slavery: Southern State Penal Systems, 1865-1890. *Social Problems*, 30(5), 555-569.

Ashforth, Blake & Mael, Fred. (1989). Social Identity Theory and Organization. *The Academy of Management Review*. 14. pp. 20-39. 10.5465/AMR.1989.4278999.

Baumer, E. P. (2007). Social Organization and Instrumental Crime: Assessing the Empirical Validity of Classic and Contemporary Anomie Theories. *Criminology*, 45(3), 617-663.

Bueno, M. (2018). *Reformed: Memoir of a Juvenile Killer.* (M. Bueno, Ed.) Detroit, Michigan: Phoenix Rising.

Covey, S. (2004). *The 7 Habits of Highly Effective People.* New York: Simon & Schuster.

Du Bois, W. (2013). *Black Reconstruction in America.* New York: Routledge.

Durose, Matthew R. (2014) *Recidivism of Prisoners released in 30 states in 2005: Patterns from 2005 to 2010.* Office of Justice Programs. Chicago: U.S. Department of Justice.

Education, U. D. (2018, October 7). Federal Student Aid. Retrieved from Studentaid. ed.gov: https://studentaid.ed.gov/sa/fafsa

Gilmore, K. (2000). Slavery and Prison - Understanding the Connections. Social Justice, 27(3 (81) *Critical Resistance to the Prison - Industrial Complex*, 195-205.

Goleman, D. (1995). *Emotional Intelligence: why it can matter more than IQ.* New Delhi: Bloomsbury.

Hallett, M. A. (2003). *Slavery's Legacy? Private Prisons and Mass Imprisonment.* In J. Marvin D. Free, *Racial Issues in Criminal Justice: The Case of African Americans.* Westport, CT, United States: Praeger Publishers.

Hamm, M. S. (2013). *The Spectacular Few: Prisoner Radicalization and the Evolving Terrorist Threat.* New York: University Press.

Hill, N. (2008). *The Law of Success: The Master Wealth-Builder's Complete and Original Lesson Plan for Achieving Your Dreams.* New York: The Penguin Group.

Kirk, D. S. (2016, May 1). *Prisoner Reentry and the Reproduction of Legal Cynicism.* Oxford Academic, 63(2), 222-243.

Liburd, D. A. (2017). *The New American Slavery: Capitalism and the Ghettoization of American Prisons as a Profitable Corporate Business.* City University of New York, Graduate Center. New York: CUNY Academic Works.

Mariel, P. a. (2018). 2018 *Update on Prisoner Recidivism A 9-Year Follow-up Period* (2005-2014). U.S. Department of Justice, Office of Justice Programs. Washington, D.C.: U.S. Department of Justice Office of Programs Bureau of Justice Statistics.

Merriam-Webster, Incorporated. (2016). *Merriam-Webster's Collegiate Dictionary* (Vol. 12). Martinsburg, WV, United States: An Encyclopedia Britannica Company.

Merton, R. K. (1948). *The Self-Fulfilling Prophecy.* The Antioch Review, 8(2), 193-210.

Puchalsk, Christina B. F.-G.-B.-P. (2009). Improving the Quality of Spiritual Care as a Dimension of Palliative Care. *Journal of Palliative Medicine,* 885-904.

Schiraldi, V., & Ziedenberg, J. (2002). *Cellblocks or Classrooms? The Funding of Higher Education and Corrections and Its Impact on African American Men.* Justice Policy Institute. Washington, D.C.: Justice Policy Institute.

Schneider, D. M. (1980). *American kinship: A cultural account.* Chicago: University of Chicago Press.

Thomas, Eric. https://etinspires.com/home

Societal Problems

Glorification of Substance Abuse Amongst Celebrities

Christiaan. "Effects of drugs on a family and information about Drug Abuse." *Families South Africa,* January 15, 2018, https://www.famsaupt.co.za/effects-of-drugs-on-a-family-and-information-about-drug-abuse/

Elkins, Chris. "Which Celebrities Have Battled with Addiction?" *Drug Rehab*, February 20, 2020, https://www.drugrehab.com/addiction/celebrities/

Kosoglou, Arianna. "Drug Glorification in Pop Culture: The Addiction Behind Your Television Screen." *Royal Life Centers*, April 16, 2019, https://royallifecenters.com/drug-glorification-in-pop-culture-the-addiction-behind-your-television-screen/

Lathan, S. Robert. "Celebrities and substance abuse." *National Center for Biotechnology Information*, October 22, 2009, https://www.ncbi.nlm.nih.gov/pmc/articles/PMC2760168/

"List of Drug Related Celebrity Deaths." *Pharmaceutical Drug Manufacturers*, http://www.pharmaceutical-drug-manufacturers.com/articles/listofdrugrelated-celebritydeaths.html

"Principles of Adolescent Substance Use Disorder Treatment: A Research-Based Guide." *National Institute on Drug Abuse*, January 2014, https://www.drugabuse.gov/publications/principles-adolescent-substance-use-disorder-treatment-research-based-guide/introduction

The Effects of Substance Abuse within the African American Community

Broman, Clifford L., Harold W. Neighbors, Jorge Delva, Myriam Torres, James S. Jackson. "Prevalence of Substance Use Disorders Among African Americans and Caribbean Blacks in the National Survey of American Life." *National Center for Biotechnology Information*, June 2008, https://www.ncbi.nlm.nih.gov/pmc/articles/PMC2377285/

Burgess, Beth. "How to Help Your Cocaine-Addicted Friend." *Healthfully*, August 14, 2017, https://healthfully.com/217788-how-to-help-your-cocaine-addicted-friend.html

Kaliszewski, Michael. "Alcohol and Drug Abuse Among African Americans." *American Addictions Centers*, July 29, 2020, https://american.addictioncenters.org/rehab-guide/addiction-statistics/african-americans

Turner, William L., Michael J. Hench. "African-American Substance Use Epidemiology and Prevention Issues", in Handbook of Drug Abuse Prevention. Handbooks of

Sociology and Social Research, pp 381-391. *Springer*, https://link.springer.com/chapter/10.1007%2F0-387-35408-5_19

"African Americans Often Face Challenges Accessing Substance Use Treatment." *Pew Trusts*, March 26, 2020, https://www.pewtrusts.org/en/research-and-analysis/articles/2020/03/26/african-americans-often-face-challenges-accessing-substance-use-treatment

"Top 5 Ways to Prevent Substance Abuse." *American Addiction Centers*, January 25, 2022, https://treatmentsolutions.com/blog/top-5-ways-to-prevent-substance-abuse/

"Why is adolescence a critical time for preventing drug addiction?" *National Institute on Drug Abuse*, July 2020, https://nida.nih.gov/publications/drugs-brains-behavior-science-addiction/preventing-drug-misuse-addiction-best-strategy

Undiagnosed Developmental and Learning Disabilities and Lack of Securing Proper Support

Bigelow, Brian J. "There's an elephant in the room: The impact of early poverty and neglect on intelligence and common learning disorders in children, adolescents, and their parents," in *Developmental Disabilities Bulletin*, 2006, Vol. 34, No. 1 & 2, pp. 177-215, https://files.eric.ed.gov/fulltext/EJ815717.pdf

Miller, Caroline. "What Is Auditory Processing Disorder?" *Child Mind Institute*, https://childmind.org/article/what-is-auditory-processing-disorder/

Novoa, Christina. "The Child Care Crisis Disproportionately Affects Children with Disabilities." *The Center for American Progress*, January 29, 2020, https://www.americanprogress.org/issues/early-childhood/reports/2020/01/29/479802/child-care-crisis-disproportionately-affects-children-disabilities/

Schechter, Julia Silverman. "Supporting the needs of students with undiagnosed disabilities." *Phi Delta Kappan*, October 22, 2018, https://kappanonline.org/schechter-supporting-needs-students-undiagnosed-disabilities/

"Clinical Profiles and Socio-Demographic Characteristics of Adults with Specific Learning Disorder in Northern Greece," in Brain Sciences, vol. 11, issue 5. MDPI Journals, March 27, 2021, https://www.mdpi.com/2076-3425/11/5/602/htm

"Consequences of Child Abuse and Neglect." *National Center for Biotechnology Information,* 2014, https://www.ncbi.nlm.nih.gov/books/NBK195987/

"Teaching Strategies: Learning Disabilities." *Walters State Community College,* https://www.ws.edu/student-services/disability/teaching/learning.shtm

"Types of Learning Disabilities." *Learning Disabilities Association of America,* https://ldaamerica.org/types-of-learning-disabilities/

"Visual Perceptual and Visual Motor Deficit Disorder." *St. Louis Learning Disabilities Association,* https://ldastl.org/about/visual-perceptual-and-visual-motor-deficit-disorder/

"What is Dyslexia?" *Understood,* https://www.understood.org/articles/en/what-is-dyslexia

"What is a Learning Disability?" *National Institute for Learning Development,* https://www.nild.org/families/what-is-a-learning-disability/

Absentee Parents

Aggarwal-Schifellite, Manisha. "Two-parent homes aren't the key for all." *The Harvard Gazette,* January 15, 2020, https://news.harvard.edu/gazette/story/2020/01/why-single-parent-homes-affect-children-differently/

Livingston, Gretchen. About one-third of U.S. children are living with an unmarried parent." *Pew Research Center,* April 27, 2018, https://www.pewresearch.org/fact-tank/2018/04/27/about-one-third-of-u-s-children-are-living-with-an-unmarried-parent/

"The Rise of Single Parent Households: Effects, Risks and Available Assistance." *Aurora University,* June 24, 2016, https://online.aurora.edu/single-parent-households/

Violence

Paul, Stan. "The Connection Between Poverty, Inequality and Firearm Violence." *UCLA Luskin School of Public Affairs,* February 1, 2017, https://luskin.ucla.edu/connection-poverty-inequality-firearm-violence

Ramos, Jose Gabriel. "Estimating The Effect of Poverty on Violent Crime." *University of North Dakota*, January 2014, https://commons.und.edu/cgi/viewcontent.cgi?article=2697&context=theses

"Violence and Abuse in Rural America." *Rural Health Information Hub*, March 26, 2021, https://www.ruralhealthinfo.org/topics/violence-and-abuse